CHARACTER
ENCYCLOPEDIA

Written by Eric Hardie

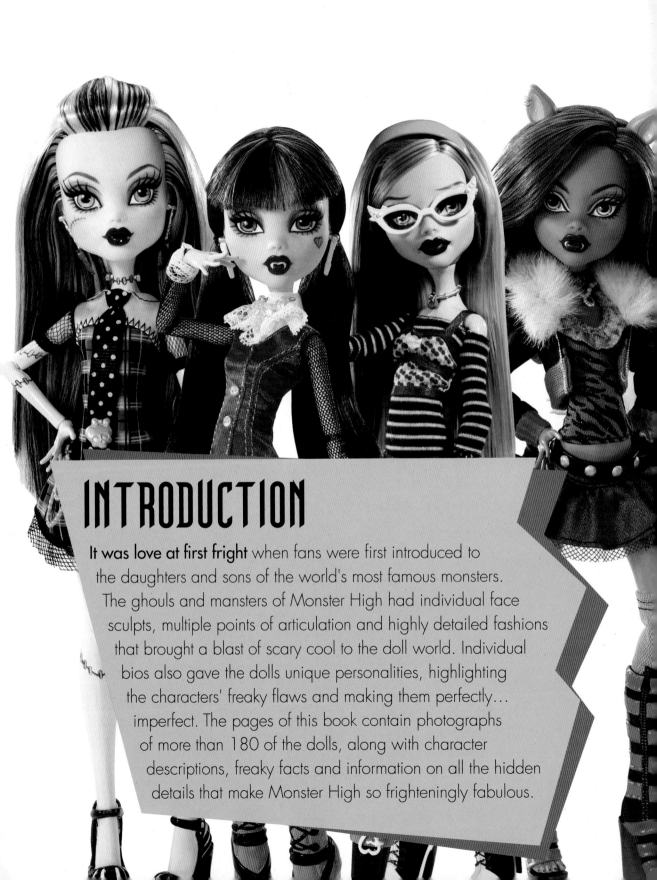

INTRODUCTION

It was love at first fright when fans were first introduced to the daughters and sons of the world's most famous monsters. The ghouls and mansters of Monster High had individual face sculpts, multiple points of articulation and highly detailed fashions that brought a blast of scary cool to the doll world. Individual bios also gave the dolls unique personalities, highlighting the characters' freaky flaws and making them perfectly… imperfect. The pages of this book contain photographs of more than 180 of the dolls, along with character descriptions, freaky facts and information on all the hidden details that make Monster High so frighteningly fabulous.

CONTENTS

FRANKIE STEIN
Stitched together with style

Frankie came to life in her father's lab, as an instant teenager. Her enthusiasm for learning new things sometimes lands her in stressful situations, causing her limbs to fly off and sparks to shoot from her bolts.

Black-and-white streaked hair

Electric-blue Skullette earrings

Coming undone
Sometimes Frankie's stitches come loose at the worst moments. At fearleading tryouts, her arm flew off and landed in front of the most creeperific guy at Monster High!

Skullette tie tack

Studded belt with lightning-bolt buckle

Tartan school ghoul uniform dress

Quilted handbag with studded straps

"My scary-cute clothes are absolutely to die for."

Watzit

AGE: How many days has it been?

DAUGHTER OF: Frankenstein

KILLER STYLE: Frankie has a keen (blue and green) eye for fashion!

FREAKY FLAW: Frankie's eyes are different colours because she was assembled from multiple body parts!

BFFs: Draculaura, Clawdeen Wolf

PET: Watzit

Black-and-white shoes match hair

DRACULAURA
Vegetarian vampire

Draculaura is the daughter of the famous vampire Count Dracula. She is bright, cheerful and full of unlife. Draculaura's favourite colour is pink. She is a strict vegetarian who faints at the sight of blood!

AGE: 1,600

DAUGHTER OF: Dracula

KILLER STYLE:
Black outfits with a splash of cheery pink.

FREAKY FLAW:
Not being able to see her own reflection can cause make-up mishaps!

BFFs: Frankie Stein, Clawdeen Wolf

PET: Count Fabulous

Safety-pin earrings

Metallic pink top with ruffle collar

Pleated school ghoul skirt

Mesh tights

Bat-handle parasol to protect skin from the sun

Pink lace-up boots with heart detail

Sculpted skull top

Count Fabulous

FREAKY FACT
Count Fabulous is an ancient vampire who is stuck in bat form. But Draculaura just thinks he's a cute bat!

9

CLAWDEEN WOLF
A wolf in chic clothing

Clawdeen is from a large pack of siblings, most of whom attend Monster High, too. She has managed to claw out a unique place for herself by being the most fiercely opinionated, fiercely loyal and fiercely fashionable ghoul at Monster High.

Pink tank top with sparkly tiger stripes

Crop jacket with faux fur collar

Purple gem pendant

Handbag with zip details

Purple miniskirt with mesh lining

AGE: 15

DAUGHTER OF:
The Werewolf

KILLER STYLE:
She's a fabulous fashionista with a confident, no-nonsense attitude.

FREAKY FLAW:
She spends too much time shaving the hair on her werewolf legs.

BFFs: Draculaura, Frankie Stein

PET: Crescent

Knee-high, peach toeless socks

"I'm howling with excitement about the new scare-mester."

Open-toed, platform sandal boots

FREAKY FACT

Clawdeen's nickname for Crescent is "Alpha Kitty".

Crescent

10

LAGOONA BLUE
Floating through unlife

Pretty pink flower hair clip

Gold sunken-treasure earrings

Gold seahorse necklace

Fish-scale swimsuit

Casual board shorts with fishnet detail on legs

Fishbowl bag, for "walking" her pet piranha, Neptuna

Fin on calf

High wedge flip-flops

Lagoona came to Monster High from down under... the sea! Captain of both the swim and surf teams, Lagoona has a laid-back, caring nature that means that her friends always go to her when they get caught up in the storms of high-school life.

FREAKY FACT
Lagoona is passionate about the environment. She cares deeply about aquatic animals and wishes that the ocean wasn't so dirty.

AGE: 15

DAUGHTER OF: The Sea Monster

KILLER STYLE: She prefers to blend into the background in muted greens and greys.

FREAKY FLAW: Her skin gets dry if she's out of the water for too long, so she goes through a lot of monsturiser.

BFFs: Lagoona is every ghoul's friend!

PET: Neptuna

11

CLEO DE NILE
You can't keep her royalty under wraps

Elaborate gold earrings

Sheer, turquoise halter-wrap top

Bandage sleeve wrap

Gold studded belt

Strapless, bandage jumpsuit

Bandage strap wedges

Cleo is the daughter of an Ancient Egyptian pharaoh, which makes her a real princess – although at Monster High she often acts like she is queen! Despite this, Cleo knows that no royal command is as powerful as the support of her friends.

"As a member of royalty, it is my duty to set a scary-good example at Monster High."

AGE:
5,842
(give or take a few years)

DAUGHTER OF: The Mummy

KILLER STYLE: Headdress, exotic jewellery and the occasional stray bandage wrap

FREAKY FLAW: Being afraid of the dark – even though she's a monster!

BFFs: Deuce Gorgon, Ghoulia Yelps

PET: Hissette

FREAKY FACT
Hissette's favourite place to sleep is in the toes of Cleo's best-loved shoes.

Hissette

12

DEUCE GORGON
Ready to rock

Deuce inherited both his snake hair and his ability to turn creatures to stone from his mom, Medusa. Deuce's laid-back attitude is only affected by the two great passions in his life – cooking and Cleo de Nile.

Snake-hawk

Silver-striped vest jacket

Green scales tattoo

Skull and cassette graphic shirt

AGE: 16

SON OF: Medusa

KILLER STYLE: Skate shoes, hoodies and his signature shades. He also rocks the snake-hawk.

FREAKY FLAW: Turning his friends temporarily to stone – but he keeps his shades on to avoid this happening.

BFFs: Cleo de Nile, Jackson Jekyll

PET: Perseus

"When I turn someone to stone, they don't stay that way – that's my mom, okay?"

Black trousers with silver scale graphics

Perseus

Stony gaze
Deuce is rarely seen without his shades. If he lifts them up, his eyes glow and flash. That's the sign for his friends to hide – or risk being turned to stone!

Chequerboard skate shoes

13

SPECTRA VONDERGEIST

A haunting beauty

Ball-and-chain earrings

Gothic-style chain bodice

Iron belt with shackles

Bucket bag with chain handle

Sparkly mesh skirt

Spectra has the ghostly ability to pass through walls and floors unseen. She uses this talent to further her career in journalism by informing all the monsters of the latest news on her blog, the *Gory Gazettte* – the most popular read at Monster High.

AGE: 16

DAUGHTER OF: The Ghosts

KILLER STYLE: Silk, silk and more silk, with a touch of metal for a spooky rattle.

FREAKY FLAW: Spectra believes that it's not healthy to focus on perceived flaws.

BFFs: Everyone loves Spectra V!

PET: Rhuen

"Being in print gives me instant credibility."

FREAKY FACT

Spectra's pet ferret, Rhuen, is also a ghost. She thinks that Rhuen is the only creature who truly understands her.

Rhuen

Translucent pink boots with chain-ball heels

14

ABBEY BOMINABLE

A warm heart in the dead of winter

Furry headband

Ice-crystal necklace

Furry arm warmers

Small bag with skeleton key

Ice-fractal patterned dress with fur collar

Abbey left her mountain home just to attend Monster High. She's tall, super strong and always gives her honest opinion. Underneath her icy exterior, Abbey has a warm heart and tries hard not to hurt her friends' feelings.

FREAKY FACT

Abbey's pet woolly mammoth, Shiver, lives with Abbey at Headmistress Bloodgood's house during term time.

Shiver

Furry snow boots

AGE:
16

DAUGHTER OF: The Yeti

KILLER STYLE: Lots of monster yak fur, which is both stylish and practical.

FREAKY FLAW: Saying exactly what she thinks. This can sometimes hurt sensitive ghouls' feelings.

BFFs: Lagoona Blue, Frankie Stein

PET: Shiver

15

GHOULIA YELPS
You can't hurry genius

Ghoulia is known throughout Monster High as the "smartest ghoul in school". She is an inventor, comic-book fan and creator, problem solver – and proof that even a zombie can stay ahead in class despite her slow speed.

Cat's-eye glasses

Ghoulia's pet owl, Sir Hoots A Lot

Zip-puller earrings

Cherry-print camisole

Fingerless fishnet gloves

Music fiend
When she hasn't got her zombie head stuck in a comic book, Ghoulia can be found listening to music. She especially likes music-inspired accessories, like her cool cassette-tape handbag.

Red polka-dot trousers with piano-key belt

Knee-high, lace-up trainer boots

"Yes we only speak Zombie, yes we slowly shuffle along, yes we often appear to be devoid of personality, but the same observation could be made about any teenager."*
*Translated from Zombie-speak

AGE: 16 – in monster years

DAUGHTER OF: The Zombies

KILLER STYLE: "Geek chic" glasses – they go with everything

FREAKY FLAW: Her zombie nature means that Ghoulia walks really, really slowly

BFFs: Cleo de Nile and everyone else at Monster High

PET: Sir Hoots A Lot

HOLT HYDE
The wild side of Jackson

Holt is the kind of manster who is the unlife and soul of every party! His DJ skills are legendary, but so too is his unpredictable, fiery personality, which sometimes blazes out of control.

Flaming hair

Holt's pet chameleon, Crossfade

Skullette headphones

Black-and-white T-shirt

Red leather jacket with gold trim

AGE: 16...
he thinks

SON OF: Mr and Mrs Hyde

KILLER STYLE: Holt's style is on fire! No really – he literally has flames leaping off his body.

FREAKY FLAW: His fiery temper is not something he's proud of, and he spends a lot of time apologising for it.

BFFs: Any monsters that love his music

PET: Crossfade

Yellow belt with turntable detail

"Do you think Jackson wonders what it's like to be as scary-cool as me?"

Pinstriped trousers with flame hems

Opposites attract
The yin-yang tattoo on the back of Holt's neck represents his dual personality. As Holt Hyde, he is hot-headed with a short temper. As his human alter ego, Jackson Jekyll, he is quiet and shy.

Untied high-top trainers

17

JACKSON JEKYLL
The responsible half of Holt

Scholarly glasses

Smart blue bow tie

Chequered sweater vest

Cheerful mustard-yellow shirt

Green satchel with yin-yang design

Neatly laced trainers

Jackson appears to be the only "normie" at Monster High. Although he does his beast to keep a low profile, his obvious "humanness" cannot go unnoticed by the other students, who regard him as nice but a bit of an oddity.

AGE: 16

SON OF: Dr and Mrs Jekyll

KILLER STYLE: Plain styles that are neat, orderly and buttoned-down

FREAKY FLAW: His dual nature makes it impossible for Jackson to know if any plan he makes is ever going to come together.

BFFs: Frankie Stein, Deuce Gorgon

PET: Crossfade

"I'm half human, half monster and all teenager. There is absolutely nothing simple about my life."

Crossfade

FREAKY FACT
Jackson is as changeable as his chameleon pet, Crossfade. Jackson has no control over when he might turn into his fiery alter ego, Holt Hyde.

CLAWD WOLF
Stylish sibling of Clawdeen

Clawd is the BMOC – Big Monster On Campus. He is popular and a great athlete, but he isn't a "dumb jock". Clawd is in a relationship with Draculaura, which is unusual since werewolves and vampires have a long history of not exactly getting along!

Teal flat cap with ear holes

Houndstooth-patterned scarf

White shirt with orange crosses design

Teal belt with gold buckle

Glamorous gold watch

Pressed dark jeans

Gold hiking boots

FREAKY FACT

Rockseena is Clawd's gargoyle bulldog. She's his number one, rock-solid fan.

Rockseena

"On the field, you never want to let another monster know they hurt you... just like in real life."

AGE: 16

SON OF: The Werewolf

KILLER STYLE: Clawd's style is "casual à la Clawdeen". He always takes his stylish sister's fashion advice.

FREAKY FLAW: Clawd sheds fur... a lot!

BFFs: A pack leader can't play favourites.

PET: Rockseena

TORALEI
Always curious to see what happens next

Toralei revels in creating mischief for mischief's sake. She especially likes it when that mischief makes things difficult for those she sees as arrogant and in need of a little humility. Toralei believes unlife is always better with a touch of chaos.

Orange neckerchief

Fingerless glove

Gold belt with silver Skullette buckle

Black ripped trousers over orange leggings

Black-and-red lace-up wedges

Red-and-black cropped jacket

Sleeveless red tunic with black-and-white stripes

AGE:
15

DAUGHTER OF:
The Werecats

KILLER STYLE:
Toralei purrfers fashions that accentuate her natural feline grace.

FREAKY FLAW:
She is overly fascinated with the claw of cause and effect.

BFFs: Meowlody, Purrsephone

PET: Sweet Fangs

Sweet Fangs

"Just because we've got nine lives, doesn't mean we need to rush through this one."

FREAKY FACT
Toralei can purrfectly mimic the voices and accents of other monsters.

20

NEFERA DE NILE
Wrapped up in the past

Nefera is Cleo's older sister and next in line to her father's throne – although her haughty demeanour and demanding nature can make it seem as if she's already wearing the crown. Nefera has outward beauty, but inside she's just as insecure as everyone else.

Gold headpiece

Snake earring

Gold serpent necklace with red jewel

Bandage dress with turquoise sash

Gold serpent belt

Double-headed serpent handle on handbag

Hissing heels
Ordinary heels won't do for an ancient Egyptian princess. The heels of Nefera's shoes are blue cobras, and there are even snake prints on the soles.

"I am incomparable to any who have come before and so I will remain."

AGE: Ageless, yet three years older than Cleo

DAUGHTER OF: The Mummy

KILLER STYLE: Colours that highlight her timeless beauty, like gold or the blue of the River Nile.

FREAKY FLAW: Flawed? Who said she was flawed?

BFFs: She rules alone

PET: Azura

Azura

Bandage leg warmers

Open-toed shoes with fan design

21

OPERETTA

Hiding behind a mask of perfection

Victory-roll hairstyle

Heart-shaped mask with musical notes

Die earring

Musical Operetta initially followed in her father's operatic footsteps, until she discovered rockabilly music and the joys of playing the guitar. Operetta is an independent spirit who doesn't scare easily. She loves exploring the secret places in the catacombs under Monster High.

Bracelet with piano-key accents

Coffin-shaped guitar with spider-web pattern

Musical-note-shaped charms

Rolled-up blue jeans

AGE:
16 – in phantom years

DAUGHTER OF:
The Phantom of the Opera

KILLER STYLE:
Operetta's red, victory-roll hairdo shows her rockabilly style.

FREAKY FLAW:
She's a bit of a diva and a perfectionist.

BFFs: Holt Hyde, Deuce Gorgon

PET: Memphis "Daddy O" Longlegs

Born music fan
Underneath Operetta's eye mask is an intricate, musical note birthmark. It extends down to end in a tattoo on her left arm.

Lace-up black-and-white treble-clef heels

Memphis "Daddy O" Longlegs

GILLINGTON "GIL" WEBBER

A true manster of honour

Gil is a manster who proves still waters run deep. His parents don't approve of him dating Lagoona Blue because she's a saltwater monster, and he's a freshwater manster – but Gil knows Lagoona is the kind of ghoul worth taking a principled stand for, even if it means making some waves!

Fin styled as a Mohawk

Freshwater breathing helmet

Pineapple cup with fish-bone stirrer

Turquoise shell necklace

Turquoise board shorts with wave graphic

Webbed fingers

Spiky fins

Black flip-flops with fish-scale strap

FREAKY FACT

Gil can't extract oxygen from the air, so he wears a helmet on dry land to help him breathe.

"Lagoona really is as kind and gentle a monster as there is in the entire monsterverse, but she's as tenacious as a riptide when she wants to be."

AGE:
16

SON OF:
The River Monster

KILLER STYLE: Tank tops, board shorts and flip-flops.

FREAKY FLAW: He's afraid of the ocean monsters that live underwater.

BFFs: Lagoona Blue, Clawd Wolf

PET: None, but he cares for Lagoona's pet piranha, Neptuna.

23

C.A. CUPID
Love doesn't have to be scary

Bow-and-arrow earrings

Heart-shaped lipstick

Bone wings

Wrist-mounted crossbow

Pink, black and white dress with bow-and-arrow heart design

Heart-shaped handbag with bow-and-arrow graphic

Heart-shaped, shackled, open-toe heels

C.A. Cupid was sent to Monster High because her adoptive father, Eros, believed her matchmaking archery skills were needed there. But she's a terrible shot, so instead of using her bow and arrows to help the students find love, Cupid fires off love advice on her daily radio show.

AGE:
As old as teenage love

DAUGHTER OF: Eros

KILLER STYLE: Lots of lace and delicate, frilly fabrics.

FREAKY FLAW: Her archery skills. Her love advice is usually more on target than her arrows.

BFFs: Any monster who is in love with love.

PET: None

"Anyone who happened to be on the archery range when I showed up to practice usually found another place they had to be, and quickly."

FREAKY FACT
C.A. Cupid would love to have a pet, but she says that there are too many fish in the sea – how could she choose just one?!

ROCHELLE GOYLE
Eternal beauty set in stone

Rochelle's gargoyle nature means her decisions are set in stone. She rarely makes them in haste and once she has made up her mind, it's difficult to change her mind. Rochelle is a strong and steadfast friend who can be more than a little bit overprotective.

FREAKY FACT

Rochelle is made from stone, so she can't do certain school activities, like swimming. It also means she is immune to Deuce Gorgon's stare, which turns people to stone!

Black, wrought-iron twist hairband

Small, stone wings

Stained-glass-effect reflective skirt

Fleur-de-lis bag clasp

AGE: 415

DAUGHTER OF:
The Gargoyles

KILLER STYLE:
Rochelle loves to mix sturdy wrought iron and pretty stained glass together.

FREAKY FLAW: She's very protective of her friends, and sometimes gets in the way when she's not needed.

BFFs: Ghoulia Yelps, Robecca Steam, Venus McFlytrap

PET: Roux

Roux

Pink mesh socks

Stone-carved, peep-toe heels

25

VENUS MCFLYTRAP

Plant and planet protector

Venus has a close connection to the earth, which is understandable for a monster who gets her sustenance directly from water, soil and the sun. Venus can get frustrated with monsters who aren't as passionate about protecting the planet as she is.

Neon pink undercut

Eco-punk Skullette motif

Canvas bag with "I heart Earth" graphics

Vine-and-chequerboard-print leggings

Vine leg warmers

Fluorescent pink, lace-up heels with sculpted teeth

AGE:
15

DAUGHTER OF:
The Plant Monster

KILLER STYLE:
Venus is bright, loud and in-your-face! She's no shrinking violet when it comes to fashion.

FREAKY FLAW:
Venus uses her pollens of persuasion to get monsters to volunteer for her eco-cause.

BFFs: Lagoona Blue, Gillington "Gil" Webber

PET: Chewlian

"Mom always says, 'Be a flower, not a weed.' Of course, the difference between a flower and a weed depends on the gardener."

FREAKY FACT
Venus can exhale her pollen onto a monster to manipulate their thoughts and actions.

Chewlian

26

ROBECCA STEAM
A scaredevil with style

Robecca is an analogue robotic monster. Built by her father during the Age of Steam, she was disassembled for a hundred years until Ghoulia Yelps found and repaired her. Robecca is often confused by the world she now lives in, but her ghoulfriends are always there to help out.

Copper flying goggles

Captain Penny

AGE:
1600

DAUGHTER OF:
Hexiciah Steam

KILLER STYLE:
Robecca describes her style as "old-fashioned", but her friends tell her it's totally "steampunk".

FREAKY FLAW:
Her internal clock doesn't work properly, so she is never on time... for anything!

BFFs: Rochelle Goyle, Frankie Stein

PET: Captain Penny

Blue metal cage skirt

Blue-and-black dress with gear graphics

Pendulum clock handbag

Copper lace-up rocket boots

Thrusters on soles and heels

Full steam ahead
Robecca can reach frightening speeds with her steam-powered boots. They have helped her become the Skultimate Roller Maze World Champion. The boots on Robecca's "Ghouls Alive" doll variant even flame at the soles.

27

MEOWLODY
A dose of purrfection

Black-and-white striped lock of hair

Meowlody is the white-maned twin sister of Purrsephone. Although at times they appear to act as one creature, Meowlody is in fact the bolder of the two, and is more likely to take the lead in making decisions for the pair.

Sleeveless, high-collared jacket

FREAKY FACT

Some monsters think that Meowlody and Purrsephone are related to Toralei because she's a werecat, too. They're not, but the trio are BFFs and are known as the worst troublemakers at Monster High!

Yarn-ball handbag

Red fingerless glove

"I like the chaos that being a twin sometimes causes. I think it's awfully clawesome and who cares if other monsters get us mixed up?"

AGE:
15

DAUGHTER OF:
The Werecats

KILLER STYLE:
Meowlody purrfers skirts, vests and shiny, jingly bracelets.

FREAKY FLAW:
She likes to play pranks that sometimes backfire.

BFFs: Toralei, Purrsephone

Bows along length of boot

Red wedge heel

PURRSEPHONE
Another dose of purrfection

Hair is the reverse of her sister's

White facial marking

Red denim miniskirt

Werecat tail

Striped leg markings

Black lace-up platform boots

Purrsephone is the dark-maned twin sister of Meowlody. Most monsters think they have identical personalities, but Purrsephone is much shyer than her twin. She sometimes has reservations about Meowlody's troublemaking plans, but she always goes along with them.

AGE:
15

DAUGHTER OF:
The Werecats

KILLER STYLE:
The same as Meowlody – it's a twin thing!

FREAKY FLAW:
Sometimes her curiosity gets her into trouble – just like Meowlody!

BFFs: Toralei, Meowlody

FREAKY FACT
Shh! It's a secret outside the family, but Purrsephone is allergic to birds – they make her sneeze and itch. They also cause hair balls, which she is extremely embarrassed about!

HOWLEEN WOLF
Howling at her own moon!

Sleeveless, paw-print hoodie

Yellow arm cuff

Paw-print embossed backpack

"H" for Howleen keychain

Multicoloured striped sock

Pink mesh sock

Black wedges with blue straps

Howleen is the youngest sister from the very large Wolf family, and because of this she is always looking for ways to stand out. Howleen is always reinventing herself, but her Monster High friends accept her no matter who she wants to be!

" ...My parents are always telling me that I'm the best at being who I am, and that Clawdeen could never beat me at being me..."

AGE:
14

DAUGHTER OF:
The Werewolves

KILLER STYLE:
Howleen likes to call her style "were-punk".

FREAKY FLAW:
Her hair. Sometimes it does what she wants, but often it does what it wants!

BFFs: Abbey Bominable, Twyla

PET: Cushion

Cushion

FREAKY FACT

Cushion's right ear is constantly folded over, just like Howleen's! They also both have the same Mohawk hairstyle.

SKELITA CALAVERAS

Kindness to the bone

Traditional Day of the Dead make-up

Skelita's role models and closest friends are members of her family. She loves the Hexican traditions that she has groan up with and seeks to genuinely share the joy of that community with every monster around her.

Grey floral and Skullette patterned top

AGE: 15

DAUGHTER OF:
Los Eskeletos

KILLER STYLE:
A mix of traditional Hexican clothing and modern fashions.

FREAKY FLAW:
She gets a chill in her bones when something is about to happen, but can't predict exactly when it will occur.

BFFs: Jinafire Long, Clawdeen Wolf

Brown leather bracelet matches belt

Multilayered, multicoloured, multi-patterned skirt

Bone legs

Hidden honour
Skelita's style is associated with Day of the Dead, a Mexican holiday for remembering loved ones who have died. She even has "Katrina" written on the back of her skull. This is in honour of the female skeleton skull that often features in Day of the Dead celebrations, *La Calavera Catrina*.

Green ribcage wedges

JINAFIRE LONG
Fire-breathing fashionista

Golden chrysanthemum hair decoration

Dragon tail

Orange tassels on ornate hair stick

Gold belt with Skullette pendant

Flame-and-cloud-print dress

Gold, scaly skin

Soles are dragon talons gripping orbs

Jinafire has seven older brothers in her Chinese Dragon family. As a result, she has developed the strong will of someone who has to fight to be included, and the calm attitude of someone who has seen far too much chaos to be surprised by anything.

FREAKY FACT
Jinafire is a talented fashion designer, and her favourite art medium is metal. She uses her fire-breathing ability to make amazing metalwork sculptures.

AGE:
1,500 scales

DAUGHTER OF:
The Chinese Dragon

KILLER STYLE:
Traditional fashions fired up with sharp cuts and fierce accessories.

FREAKY FLAW:
She is strong-willed and hot tempered – a dangerous combination around combustible material!

BFFs: Skelita Calaveras, Clawdeen Wolf

TWYLA
A bootiful dreamer

Eyes glow in the dark

Handbag with dreamcatcher clasp

Bracelet with skull-shaped dreamcatcher

Layered skirt with swirling dust-cloud design

Swirling clouds of grey dust

Dust-mite laces

Ankle boots with dust-devil heels

Twyla is the kind of ghoul who does her beast to stay out of the spotlight – literally! Her ability to jump from shadow to shadow without being seen is very useful, as Twyla is extremely shy.

AGE:
15

DAUGHTER OF:
The Boogey Man

KILLER STYLE:
Twyla loves dark blues and deep purples that blend in with the shadows.

FREAKY FLAW:
She's painfully shy, so it's difficult for her to make new friends.

BFFs: Howleen Wolf, Spectra Vondergeist

PET: Dustin

FREAKY FACT
Twyla's dust bunny, Dustin, is very sensitive to gusts of wind, so he spends most of his time indoors.

Dustin

GIGI GRANT

As you wish

Gigi received a new lease of unlife when Howleen Wolf used a wish to free her from a lantern, where she was trapped as a genie, granting wishes. Now the opportunity to experience and explore what she once could only wish for has given Gigi a contagious sense of optimism.

Ponytail resembles a scorpion's tail

Tapered fingers with long nails

Ornate scorpion tattoo

Scorpion bracelets match earrings

Gold arachnid detail on trousers

AGE: 15

DAUGHTER OF: The Genie

KILLER STYLE:
Natural fabrics, especially silk, in bright colours.

FREAKY FLAW:
Being stuck in a lantern has made Gigi very claustrophobic!

BFFs: She wishes she could name even one!

PET: Sultan Sting

"I will never understand the desire... to wish for more wishes. A) It never works and B) It really annoys your genie."

Sultan Sting

FREAKY FACT

Gigi loves outer space and her favourite subject is astronomy.

Platform slippers with upturned toes

HEADLESS HEADMISTRESS BLOODGOOD
Monster High Head

Headless Headmistress Bloodgood started Monster High with five ghouls in a rented mausoleum and a dream – a dream that one day monsters of all kinds could come together under one roof to be educated. Many years have passed since then, and she has seen her dream come true.

The Headmistress's head sometimes sits here

Collared shirt with pink tie

Pink and red cuffs

Headless Headmistress's head

AGE: Wise enough to be your grandmother – young enough to be your sister.

DAUGHTER OF: The Headless Horseman

KILLER STYLE: Riding coat, high-collared blouse, riding boots, yardstick and a book on grammar.

FREAKY FLAW: Sometimes her head and her body find themselves in different places!

BFFs: She is content with her own company and a good book.

PET: Nightmare

Purple and pink riding coat with gold buttons

Black riding boots

FREAKY FACT
Headmistress Bloodgood speaks 10 languages, including Ancient Werewolf, Gorgon, Troll and Dragon.

Nightmare

35

CATRINE DEMEW
Drawn into Monster High

Catrine is a Scarisian werecat and street artist. After meeting many of the Monster High ghouls while they were in Scaris, Catrine decided to leave her beloved city to attend Monster High, too. Of course, she brought all of her art supplies with her just in case there's time to sketch between classes!

Striped, princess-sleeve T-shirt

Scarf with wrought-iron detail

Wrought-iron handle

Painting of Scaris on purse

AGE: 415

DAUGHTER OF:
A Werecat

KILLER STYLE: The latest Scarisian fashions – they help frame her artistic abilities.

FREAKY FLAW:
Being a purrfectionist sometimes makes it difficult for her to finish her sketches.

BFFs: Scaris! The city is always with her.

"Packing is going to be très difficile because the more clothes I bring, the more art supplies I must leave."

Artistic fashion
Catrine has always been passionate about art. When she was younger she would spend her free time prowling the Scaris pavements as a street artist. She never leaves the house without her art supplies – even the heels of her shoes are paintbrushes!

Platforms with chalk stack soles

CATTY NOIR
The siren of superstition

International pop star Catty traded in a charmed life of fame and fortune to be an ordinary ghoul at Monster High. Many monsters thought this was a publicity stunt, but Catty didn't want to miss the experience of high school, and swapped her concert schedule for a class one!

Sleek, hot pink hair

Hot pink, broken-glass necklace

Metallic cordless mic with Skullette detail

Studded pink bangle

Silver broken-mirror dress

Sparkly tulle skirt

Silver broken-mirror platform boots

AGE: 16

DAUGHTER OF: A Werecat

KILLER STYLE: Flashy, larger than unlife outfits – they're ghoulishly glitzy and creeperifically cool!

FREAKY FLAW: Catty's unlife decisions are dictated by her many superstitions.

BFFs: She's looking forward to making some at Monster High!

FREAKY FACT
Catty won her first talent contest as a singer when she was seven years old.

37

INVISI BILLY

Now you see him... you know the rest

Blue beanie

Messenger bandolier

Bike-lock necklace

Silver paracord bracelet

Cut-off blue jeans

White-and-black loafers

Invisi Billy loves being a prankster. Fortunately, he has a good nature, so the pranks are never of the mean-spirited variety. That's not to say his ability to appear and disappear at will isn't a source of exasperation – especially to the school photographer on picture day!

AGE: 15

SON OF:
The Invisible Man

KILLER STYLE:
Billy unlives in his hoodie, cut-off jeans and beanie. He calls this look "blipster".

FREAKY FLAW:
Sometimes he uses his invisibility to avoid problems, instead of dealing with them.

BFFs: Scarah Screams, Catty Noir

"I am not a ghost, or a spirit, or a phantom. I am invisible."

FREAKY FACT
When he leaves school, Billy wants to follow in his father's footsteps and do special effects for movies.

SLOMAN "SLO MO" MORTAVITCH

Tall, dark and zombie

"Slo Mo" is the kind of manster who moves at his own pace, regardless of what is going on around him. It's not just because he's a zombie, either – even his ghoulfriend, Ghoulia, acknowledges that Sloman earned his nickname fair and square.

High-top fade hairstyle

Monster High pennant

Purple Monster High logo T-shirt

Casual jean shorts with white stitching

FREAKY FACT

Ghoulia says that no monster can beat Sloman at chess, not even her.

"Ghoulia tells me I make decisions slower than a glacier moves."*

*Translated from Zombie-speak

AGE: 16

SON OF: The Zombies

KILLER STYLE:
Sloman keeps his style decisions simple: jeans, T-shirt, trainers and a jacket.

FREAKY FLAW:
He must have all the facts before he makes any decisions – all of them!

BFFs: Ghoulia Yelps, Deuce Gorgon

High-top casketball shoes

HEATH BURNS

A fiery personality

Flame-shaped hair

Heath's fiery powers are hard to control, and he tends to act on impulse – with unfortunate consequences for those around him. Despite the chaos caused by Heath's poor decisions, he has a good heart and always does his beast to make amends.

Marshmallow roasting stick

Athletic shirt with flame graphics

Blue jean shorts

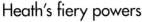

FREAKY FACT

Heath Burns is Jackson Jekyll/Holt Hyde's first cousin. Uncontrollable powers clearly run in the family!

AGE:
15

SON OF:
The Fire Elementals

KILLER STYLE:
The Heathster knows the other mansters at Monster High take their style cues from him, so he keeps it casual.

FREAKY FLAW:
He bursts into flames at the worst moments!

BFFs: Deuce Gorgon, Clawd Wolf

"I have lots of accidents. The emergency room has a seat with my name on it. Honestly, it's a little plaque that says 'Reserved for Heath Burns'."

Orange hiking boots

JANE BOOLITTLE
It's a jungle out there!

Jane has no memory of before the time Dr Boolittle found her running wild in the jungle at the age of five or six. What she does know is that she can speak to and understand animals. Jane's not sure where this ability came from, she's just always had it!

Feather and Skullette headband

Three-ringed choker

Bone and feather earrings

Tank top with floral print

Fang, feather and Skullette voodoo belt

Padded medicine bag

Secret keeper
Years spent living in the jungle, with only the animals as friends, have made Jane a great listener. She knows how to keep a secret, and when words fail her, she uses the hidden pen in her staff to write secret messages.

Staff with red-ribboned Skullette

Leggings with serrated edges

Mismatched, tribal boot wedges

AGE:
15 or 16

DAUGHTER OF:
Dr Boolittle

KILLER STYLE:
Jane calls her style "jungle chic". She adores faux fur, feathers and animal prints.

FREAKY FLAW:
She gets panicky when she's in a large group of monsters.

BFFs: Jane is a friend to any animal in need

PET: Needles

Needles

VIPERINE GORGON
The scare and make-up artist

With her striking pink locks and vivacious personality, Viperine is a ghoul who is comfortable in her own scales. This serves her well in her job as the scare and make-up artist for some of Hauntlywood's biggest stars, who swear that her work can take 400 years off them!

Serpent headband

Pink-tinted serpent shades

Slithering serpent necklace

Six serpent locks

Paisley-print dress with ruffled hem

Scaly skin

Lace-up wedge boots with writhing snakes

AGE:
17

DAUGHTER OF: Stheno (steth-an-uh), Sister of Medusa

KILLER STYLE:
Hippie booho chic that mixes patterns, colours and fabrics.

FREAKY FLAW:
Viperine tends to show affection with bites rather than hugs... she's working on this!

BFFs: Elissabat, Honey Swamp

Practice makes perfect
Viperine has monster make-up skills and her make-up box is her prized possession – she takes it with her everywhere. She loves practising her make-up skills on her friends.

"Sometimes, I go to the elder monsters' home and do makeovers for the monsters that live there. They have great stories to tell and I get to hear them. It's a win win."

42

HONEY SWAMP
Frightfully focused

Pink sun hat with decorative flower

Teal and turquoise hair

Vine and monster-flower belt

Monster-flower-print dress with shredded hemline

Swamp vines

Pink wedge heels with sculpted alligator detail

Aspiring cinematographer Honey is as comfortable wading through an alligator-and-snake-infested swamp looking for the perfect shot as she is entertaining guests at a formal dinner party. Honey believes that she epitomises what it means to be a modern Southern ghoul.

Following her screams
Honey has big plans for an unlife behind the camera. She captures monster moments on her handheld camera and is well on her way to making it in Hauntlywood.

AGE:
115 – in swamp monster years

DAUGHTER OF: The Honey Island Swamp Monster

KILLER STYLE:
She's sweet, mannerly, feminine and fiercely independent.

FREAKY FLAW:
She's a perfectionist, which she acknowledges can be tiresome for other monsters!

BFFs: Viperine Gorgon, Clawdia Wolf

"I am a photographer. I do not *want* to be one, you understand – I *am* one. I am always striving to learn more and be... perfect."

43

ELISSABAT
Star of the silver scream

Silky black hair with purple highlights

Elissabat is the reigning Queen of the Vampires. It's a title she wasn't eager to claim, and she spent 400 years hiding out as an actress named Veronica Von Vamp! Eventually Elissabat did take the throne, but her film legacy still inspires and entertains legions of fans.

Purple bat-wing bracelet

Lace-up bodice

Purple and black multilayered dress

"On the eve of my coronation, 400 years ago, I slipped into the moonless Transylvanian darkness and disappeared forever."

Mesh ruffle layers on skirt

Black platform wedge boots with bow detail

AGE: 1,601

DAUGHTER OF:
A Vampire

KILLER STYLE:
Lots of lace, ruffles, silk and satin – as long as it's frilly and in black or deep purple.

FREAKY FLAW:
She suffers from terrible stage fright and must be completely prepared before she stands in front of an audience.

BFFs: Draculaura, Viperine Gorgon

Boovie star
Elissabat always works hard to overcome her stage fright and give the best performance possible. She even won a clawesome award for her most recent role in Hauntlywood!

44

CLAWDIA WOLF
Chewing on a good story

Hoop earrings

Clawdia is the oldest female sibling in the Wolf family – she's also the clumsiest and least athletic. Not that it matters, for clever Clawdia has set her sights on a career as a screamwriter in Hauntlywood.

Neat corduroy blazer

Black studded bracelet

Sleeveless metallic dress with star, moon and bone print

AGE:
19

DAUGHTER OF:
The Werewolf

KILLER STYLE:
Tribal prints mixed with scholarly flare.

FREAKY FLAW:
When Clawdia is nervous or thinking hard she absent-mindedly chews on anything within reach!

BFFs: Her brothers and sisters

"...Symbolism in ghost-modern, neo-realist goblin cinema is only slightly less painful than rolling in flea-infested wolfsbane."

Knee-high socks

FREAKY FACT

Clawdia was the first Monster High doll to be sculpted with a smile.

Studded gold shoes

45

GILDA GOLDSTAG
Startling deer

Deer antler

Foam Monster High spirit claw

Large gold hoop earrings

Light-brown bolero jacket with bull's-eye motif

Forest green shirt

Orange belt with gold buckle

Dark brown faux-leather pants

Patent knee-high boots

Gilda is the kind of ghoul who always seems to be one step ahead of everyone else around her. Whether it's because she wants a head start on unlife, or because the view is better from the front, it means all of Gilda's classmates are playing catch-up!

"I hate it when monsters challenge me to a race. It's embarrassing... for them... and I don't like showing up my friends."

AGE:
19

DAUGHTER OF:
The Golden Hind

KILLER STYLE:
Gilda loves the neutral colours of nature and prefers sleek to frilly.

FREAKY FLAW:
She's a little on the nervous side, especially when it comes to sudden loud noises.

BFFs: Jane Boolittle, Venus McFlytrap

46

CASTA FIERCE
A spellbinding performer

Streaked hair quiff

Studded shoulder cage

Purple microphone

Orange puff sleeves

Casta and her band, "The Spells", spend the entire year preparing for their one-and-only concert appearance on All Hallows Eve. Monsters who have managed to score a ticket and see the show describe it as an absolutely unlife-changing event – sometimes literally!

Orange-and-purple, shimmer-finish dress

Casta's broom doubles as a microphone stand

Black-and-silver studded skirt belt

Glitter fishtail skirt

AGE: 19

DAUGHTER OF: Circe

KILLER STYLE: Lots of belts and buckles crisscrossing her favourite black-and-purple fashions.

FREAKY FLAW: Casta's lyrics can become a spell that transforms her audience into animals!

BFFs: Catty Noir, Operetta

Purple high heels with silver studs and buckles

NEIGHTHAN ROT
Clumsy cool

Neighthan is a manster you just can't help but want to succeed. He's like a clumsy, sweet character from a teen romance movie whose beast intentions always seem to result in chaos – but the goodness of Neighthan's heart always shines through!

Translucent blue unicorn horn

Yellow, blue and red streaked mane

Shirt with anatomy graphic

Spiked baseball hat with holes for ears and horn

Baggy trousers with leg muscle graphic

Yellow spiked high-top trainers

AGE: 17

SON OF: A Zombie and a Unicorn

KILLER STYLE: Spike details to match his unicorn horn and bold, bright colours that camouflage the results of his clumsiness.

FREAKY FLAW: He's so clumsy he could trip over the wind!

BFFs: Sirena Von Boo, Avea Trotter, Bonita Femur

FREAKY FACT
Neighthan can use his unicorn horn to heal injuries. But he is most likely to heal himself, because his extreme clumsiness means he is constantly tripping over things!

48

SIRENA VON BOO
Swimming spectre

Sirena moves on the invisible tides of her own thoughts. This makes her reliable when it comes to giving insightful opinions, and completely unreliable when it comes to keeping appointments! Sirena's friends know this, and even though they invite her to everything, they're always surprised when she shows up.

AGE:
17

DAUGHTER OF:
A Mermaid and
a Ghost

KILLER STYLE:
Sirena pays homage to her heritage by intertwining pearls with chains.

FREAKY FLAW:
She's a daydreamer who tends to float in whatever direction her thoughts take her.

BFFs: Avea Trotter, Bonita Femur, Neighthan Rot

FREAKY FACT
When she is on land, Sirena can often be found in antique shops, searching for pretty treasures.

Tumbling, blue hair waves

Irises are water bubbles

Silver, three-strand chain necklace

Tentacle-graphic top with black mesh ruffle

Pearl-and silver-chain tail net

Dangling loops on wristband

Mermaid tail

49

AVEA TROTTER
Taking the reins

Black headstall and top hat with red feathers

Avea's stubborn streak proves that sometimes a horse can't be led to water! Her hybrid heritage, and past experiences with monsters who have treated her poorly because of it, have increased her stubborness – but if Avea is your friend, she will be for unlife!

Wings from her harpy scaritage

Red tartan jacket with princess sleeves

Black tail wrap

FREAKY FACT

Avea would love a pet, but she has never found one that is able to keep up with her fast pace!

Black harness with horseshoe charms

AGE:
17

DAUGHTER OF:
A Harpy and a Centaur

KILLER STYLE:
Avea kicks up her heels in equestrian haunt couture.

FREAKY FLAW:
She's a little bit – okay a lot – stubborn!

BFFs: Sirena Von Boo, Bonita Femur, Neighthan Rot

Lavender Skullette dapples

Black tendon boots

BONITA FEMUR
Nervous to the bone

Bonita has a sweet and caring personality that soars – when it's not weighed down with worry, that is! Fortunately, her friends act as a calming influence on her nervous nature and when Bonita remembers to laugh and have fun, she completely forgets to worry.

Butterfly hair comb

Large, intricate wings

Yellow bone and butterfly belt

AGE:
16

DAUGHTER OF: A Skeleton and the Mothman

KILLER STYLE:
Bonita is totally attracted to bright colours.

FREAKY FLAW:
When she gets nervous, she chews on her clothes.

BFFs: Sirena Von Boo, Avea Trotter, Neighthan Rot

Yellow skeletonised heels

Moth fur

"I love art class. I'm really attracted to form and light."

51

Fluorescent green fedora hat

Bolero sweater with footprint graphics

Lime green plait tied with orange tassel tie

Monster-flower-print skirt

Coffin-shaped bag with footprint etching

Huge, pink platform wedges with green tassels

Furry shins

Marisol's feet are so huge, her toes peek out of her shoes

MARISOL COXI
Best foot forward

Marisol is not the kind of ghoul who tries to avoid standing out in a crowd – she actually loves the attention! Marisol is a force of good nature in size 42EEE wedges and, unless you have a headache, it's impossible to be gloomy when she's around.

Monstrous feet

Marisol's feet are huge in comparison to those of other monsters, but she has learned to love them. Footprints adorn all her clothes – from her bolero sweater right down to the soles of her shoes.

AGE: 17

DAUGHTER OF:
The South American Bigfoot

KILLER STYLE:
Marisol likes BIG and LOUD colours, fashion, music and hair.

FREAKY FLAW:
Her volume is stuck on loud and even her whisper is as quiet as an avalanche.

BFFs: Abbey Bominable, Lorna McNessie

LORNA MCNESSIE
A wee lass from the Loch

Plaid Tam o'Shanter cap

Red short-sleeved blouse with black diamond pattern

Celtic-knot belt with shoulder straps

Loch Ness Monster print on skirt

Spiky monster tail

Spiky fin

Sporran with moulded Celtic knots and Loch Ness Monster design

Black platform wedges with grey castle-brick heels

Lorna has spent her entire unlife trying to appear in every photo taken even remotely close to her. This is a source of both wonder and frustration among her notoriously photo-shy family, who don't want to give tourists, scientists and monster-hunters any encouragement!

AGE: 14

DAUGHTER OF:
The Loch Ness Monster

KILLER STYLE: Lorna wears her clan's tartan, wool skirts and scarfs.

FREAKY FLAW: She's a compulsive photobomber and no picture is safe from her image!

BFFs: Marisol Coxi, Gillington "Gil" Webber

Monster scaritage
Clad in her clan's tartan, it's clear for all to see that Lorna hails from bonny Rotland. She even has an intricate Celtic knot design on her torso.

53

PORTER "PAINTERGEIST" GEISS

Making monsterpieces

Collared shirt with custom pink-and-blue paint drips

Silver chain harness holds cans of ghost paint

Silver chain belt

Silver chain cuff

Shorts with brick graphics and paint stains

Translucent-blue athletic shoes

Porter wields his paint cans like a music conductor wields his baton – each stroke is precise, each flourish is purposeful. But each time he gets caught equals detention! In Porter's defence, his public art is done with fade-away ghost paint, so his detentions last longer than his monsterpieces.

"Sometimes, I think unlife would be easier if I was just a regular ghost – if there really is such a thing."

AGE:
16

SON OF:
A Poltergeist

KILLER STYLE:
Porter likes to make a fashion statement by wearing his art.

FREAKY FLAW:
He would rather spray it than say it, which isn't always appreciated by the monsters in power!

BFFs: River Styxx, Kiyomi Haunterly, Vandala Doubloons

PET: Huebert

Translucent pink pirate hat with pirate-ship hatpin

VANDALA DOUBLOONS

Ahoy, monster!

Pink bone and tentacle corset with chains

Vandala and her skeleton crew ride the winds and waves of the great haunted ocean that washes onto the shores of the ghost realm. Vandala is on a constant search for adventure, treasure – and a cure for seasickness!

Teal-and-black wave-print dress

AGE:
16

DAUGHTER OF: A Ghost Pirate

KILLER STYLE:
Nautical Yo-Ho-Bo-Ho chic

FREAKY FLAW:
She gets seasick. It's embarrassing for a pirate, and strange for a ghost!

BFFs: River Styxx, Kiyomi Haunterly

PET: A cuttlefish named Aye

Chain and anchor purse features a Skullette with an eyepatch

Intricately carved peg leg

Translucent shoe with treasure-chest heel

FREAKY FACT

Vandala's pirate ship is called the *Salty Spectre*. When she's not feeling seasick, Vandala can be found sailing the deep boo sea searching for lost treasure.

RIVER STYXX
Not so grim

Reaper's staff with lavender Skullette bow

River's infectious energy and bouncy, floaty personality make her seem more like a party planner for the "passed on" than a junior Reaper in Training – much to her father's annoyance. Any monster would have to be dead inside not to have fun when River's around!

Pink bone bow necklace

FREAKY FACT

River is a Reaper in Training (R.I.P). This means that she can only carry a staff and not a scythe (a sharp-bladed tool).

Pastel green chain bracelet with Skullette charm

Lavender chain belt with Skullette bow

Mesh hooded cape

Tie-dye Skullette-print dress

AGE:
14

DAUGHTER OF: The Grim Reaper

KILLER STYLE:
Candy colours all swirled together – so sweet it will make your bones hurt!

FREAKY FLAW: She often appears suddenly behind unsuspecting monsters.

BFFs: Vandala Doubloons, Porter "Paintergeist" Geiss

PET: A raven named Cawtion

Bones visible through lower legs

Translucent-blue lace-up boots with chain bows

KIYOMI HAUNTERLY
Faceless fashionista

Kiyomi was once just a faceless ghost in the crowd, until she discovered her ability to open portals into the non-ghost world of "the solids" at Monster High. What Kiyomi saw there unchained her inner fashionista and gave her spirit permission to soar!

AGE:
16

DAUGHTER OF:
The Noppera-bō
(faceless ghost)

KILLER STYLE:
Fashions that are comfortable and floaty for hovering.

FREAKY FLAW: She can't hide her feelings as her body literally changes colour with her emotions!

BFFs: Spectra Vondergeist, Draculaura

PET: A baby kaiju (monster)

Blue hair clip with face and cherry-blossom details

Purple sheer cape with metallic cherry blossoms

Lavender neck collar with face detail, studs and chains

Cuff features face design

Bag has ghostly face print

Pink shackle belt with face, star and cherry blossom charms

Face value
As a Noppera-bō (faceless ghost), Kiyomi has no facial features – but she has the scary-cool ability to make her face match other monsters' faces. In fact, if her shoes and other accessories are anything to go by, she's a little obsessed with faces!

Transluscent-gold shoes

57

FINNEGAN WAKE
Speedy scaredevil

Large Mohawk fin

Brown leather backpack

Skull, race flag and flame tattoo

Black, fingerless racing gloves

Flame-shaped spokes

Merman fin

Finnegan has never let life in a wheelchair confine or define him. He is a complete manster of action who is always pushing himself beyond the expectations of others, while still chasing the high expectations he has set for himself.

FREAKY FACT

Finnegan won a worldwide fan vote to be made into a Monster High doll.

"You know what's totally clawesome? When the outdoor pool at Monster High gets drained for repairs, and the workers leave the equipment ramp in the pool."

AGE:
17

SON OF:
A Merman

KILLER STYLE:
His blue Mohawk fin and clawesome tats may say "punk rocker", but Finnegan's fashions are pure race-wear

FREAKY FLAW:
He's a scaredevil who doesn't like to be told, "That's too dangerous!" even if it is.

BFFs: Gigi Grant, Lorna McNessie

KJERSTI TROLLSON
A level up on the competition

Kjersti is a Troll from Goreway, who also goes by the gamer name Trollhammer530. The fangtastic gamer spends most of her time logged into game servers, challenging other gamers across the monster world. She's only been defeated once – by a student at Monster High named Ghoulia Yelps.

"Characters in a game that do not move are targets; characters in a game that move without a plan are moving targets."

Knitted horned helmet

Pixelated irises behind pixel-frame glasses

Earrings match Skullette logo on T-shirt

Kjersti's personalised Skullette symbol has a helmet and a pixelated outline

Multicoloured pixel-print skirt

Game controller handbag

Heeled hiking boots have pixel details on soles and game controller details on laces

AGE
14 – in Troll years

DAUGHTER OF: A Troll

KILLER STYLE:
Kjersti loves giving her wardrobe a turbo boost of cute with scary-cool game themes.

FREAKY FLAW:
Kjersti is a control freak. If only real life had a game controller!

BFFS: Ghoulia Yelps, Heath Burns

59

AMANITA NIGHTSHADE
Weed between the lines

Black vine necklace

Modelling portfolio

Black petal bag with vine strap

iCoffin

Nightshade blossom and vine ankle bracelet

Sheer dress with leaf and vine pattern

Amanita believes that truly authentic beauty should always be celebrated – and if that means such a celebration should be centred on her, who is she to object? She thinks that humility is just a false emotion to make lesser monsters feel better about themselves.

AGE:
17 – in Corpse Flower Years

DAUGHTER OF:
The Corpse Flower

KILLER STYLE:
Her cultivated look makes every other flower in the garden of style look like a weed.

FREAKY FLAW:
She believes there's nothing so wonderful as the sound of her own melodic voice.

BFF: Herself!

FREAKY FACT
An Amanita is a type of poisonous mushroom and nightshades are toxic flowers.

Black vine heels

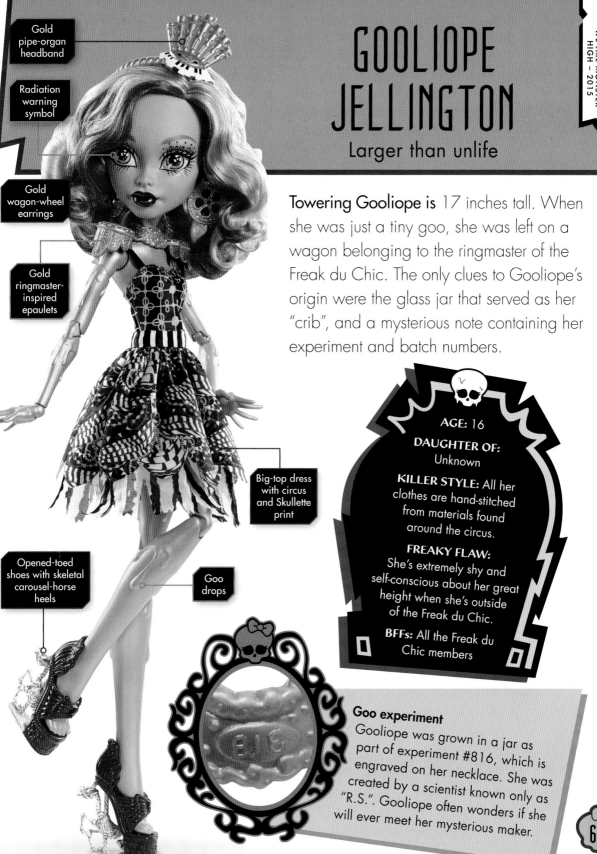

GOOLIOPE JELLINGTON

Larger than unlife

Gold pipe-organ headband

Radiation warning symbol

Gold wagon-wheel earrings

Gold ringmaster-inspired epaulets

Big-top dress with circus and Skullette print

Opened-toed shoes with skeletal carousel-horse heels

Goo drops

Towering Gooliope is 17 inches tall. When she was just a tiny goo, she was left on a wagon belonging to the ringmaster of the Freak du Chic. The only clues to Gooliope's origin were the glass jar that served as her "crib", and a mysterious note containing her experiment and batch numbers.

AGE: 16

DAUGHTER OF: Unknown

KILLER STYLE: All her clothes are hand-stitched from materials found around the circus.

FREAKY FLAW: She's extremely shy and self-conscious about her great height when she's outside of the Freak du Chic.

BFFs: All the Freak du Chic members

Goo experiment

Gooliope was grown in a jar as part of experiment #816, which is engraved on her necklace. She was created by a scientist known only as "R.S.". Gooliope often wonders if she will ever meet her mysterious maker.

61

ISI DAWNDANCER
Hooved groover

Isi may be shy by nature, but she has always been the kind of ghoul who can dance like nobody is watching. She loves any excuse to dance – whether it's to the music being pumped out across a dance floor or to the music in her head!

"Dancing with the dust devils is hard on a pedicure."

Antler headdress with pink headband and dreamcatcher

Yellow bead necklace with half-moon charm

Woven, off-the-shoulder patterned top

Pink-and-teal triangle bracelets

Teal spider-web dreamcatcher handbag

Skullette-patterned leggings

Tasselled wedge boots with pink dreamcatcher ribbon

Hoof peeking out

AGE:
16

DAUGHTER OF:
A Deer Spirit

KILLER STYLE:
Bright colours and patterns that reflect her Boo Hexican Deer Spirit heritage.

FREAKY FLAW:
She has an effect on mansters that makes them fall head over antlers for her!

BFFs: Twyla, Gilda Goldstag

BATSY CLARO
Doesn't care if it's a jungle out there

Batsy is as comfortable in the dense jungles of her native Costa Shrieka as most ghouls are shopping at the maul. She guides monsters into the jungle for her parents' ecotourism business. Watching their faces fright up at the unnatural wonder is monstrously cool.

"Some monsters should just stay in the city. 'It's too hot.' 'The bugs are biting me.' It's a jungle, for screaming out loud! What do they expect?"

Woven palm-frond headband with white bat

Bat earrings

Woven palm-frond travel bag

Intricate bat wings

Multicoloured, jungle-print shorts

Woven palm-frond wedge boots

AGE:
17

DAUGHTER OF:
The White Vampire Bat

KILLER STYLE:
Woven palm fronds and the fright colours of orchids. Batsy gets her inspiration from the jungle.

FREAKY FLAW:
She has a problem with monsters who choose to stay in the dark when it comes to protecting the environment.

BFFs: Venus McFlytrap, Jane Boolittle

63

GARROTT DUROQUE
Scarisian manster

Coiffed, electric-blue hair

Granite wings

Garrott is a fashion designer whose creativity is not set in stone – although he can be rather hard-headed when it comes to perfecting his work. Living in Scaris, the City of Frights, has given Garrott valuable first-claw experience in the fashion industry.

Spider web and rose-patterned scarf

Pet rose

AGE: 516

SON OF: A Gargoyle

KILLER STYLE:
The style basics – skinny jeans, scarf, dragon leather jacket and boots.

FREAKY FLAW:
A perfectionist to the extreme – if his designs aren't perfect, he starts all over again.

BFFs: Rochelle Goyle, Clawdeen Wolf

"She [Rochelle] was frowning, but such a frown! It was magnifique! In that frown I found my inspiration..."

Stylish skinny blue jeans

Hiking boots

Bootiful blooms
Garrott is a great gardener. He especially likes roses – he thinks of them as his pets and even talks to them! Roses provide the inspiration for all his new fashion designs, including his boots.

LUNA MOTHEWS
Fright lights, big city

Luna grew up in Boo Jersey, right across the river from Boo York, where she was always attracted to the fright lights of the big city. Luna is a talented singer, dancer and actor – she hopes to be a shockingly big star one day.

FREAKY FACT
If Luna spins around really fast, she can alter the clothes she is wearing.

Moth-shaped, metallic-orange headpiece

Moth wings

Black-and-metallic-red jumpsuit

Large Skullette on mesh train

Silver, knee-high heels with fluttering moths

AGE: 16

DAUGHTER OF: The Mothman

KILLER STYLE:
Dark fabrics with bright pops of colour – like the city at night. She is a total goth moth!

FREAKY FLAW:
Luna is easily distracted from her path to stardom by her ghoulfriends.

BFFs: Elle Eedee, Mouscedes King

65

MOUSCEDES KING
Boo York royalty

Turquoise
crystal tiara

Crystal-grey
earrings match
shoulder pads

Iridescent-grey
Swiss-cheese
shoulder pads

Mouscedes is a privileged ghoul from a family of rich Upper Beast Side monsters. She is used to being waited on and loves to be pampered. She believes that there's never an excuse for not having the very beast of everything.

AGE:
15

DAUGHTER OF: The Rat King

KILLER STYLE:
Totally Upper Beast Side!

FREAKY FLAW:
This rat ghoul can't eat regular cheese because she is lactose intolerant.

BFFs: Elle Eedee,
Luna Mothews

Rat
tail

Turquoise
crystal belt
matches tiara

Metallic cheese
and broken-
crystal print
gown

"I may come from Boo York royalty, but I'm no Upper Beast Side snob."

Rat King
Skullette

66

ELLE EEDEE
Loving the mechanics of music

Blue crystal-and-antenna headpiece

Purple crystal earrings match cape

Metallic silver circuit skirt

Elle may be a robot but the music she creates is anything but mechanical. She is machine-driven to forge a career as a professional DJ, and spends as much time as she can practicing her skills so that they don't get rusty.

"I try to keep the dancing to a minimum, because it is not good for a robot to overheat too much."

FREAKY FACT
Elle has the ability to receive and translate messages from space.

AGE:
16

DAUGHTER OF:
The Robots

KILLER STYLE:
Clean lines and shiny metallic fashions.

FREAKY FLAW:
She gets amped up when she dances and blows fuses!

BFFs: Luna Mothews, Mouscedes King

Translucent blue shoes

Purple-and-blue cape with circuit pattern

67

ASTRANOVA
Fright-years beyond everyone else

Comet-crystal microphone headset

Winged comet-crystal belt and chestpiece

Silver forearm covers

Halterneck dress with magenta constellation pattern

Knee-high, magenta crystal boots

Astranova is just your scareo-typical ghoul next door – if you measure distance between doors in light-years! Cruising through space with only the sound of her own voice and old TV shows to keep her company, Astranova was more than ready for fun when she landed on Earth.

AGE:
15 – in space years

DAUGHTER OF:
The Comet Aliens

KILLER STYLE:
Glam rock. The more sparkle and stellar shine the better!

FREAKY FLAW:
She has a difficult time understanding Earth monster slang, which can lead to misunderstandings.

BFFs: Luna Mothews, Mouscedes King, Elle Eedee

Out of this world
Astranova was lost in space when an unknown force drew her crystal comet to planet Earth. She can float down from her crystal comet towards the Boo York skyline in this playset.

KALA MER'RI

Swimming above the competition

Kala's passion for dance and competition can be seen from the roomful of trophies she has won for her monster moves. Kala loves to dance almost as much as she loves to be in control – she likes to have her tentacles on everything!

AGE:
16

DAUGHTER OF:
The Kraken

KILLER STYLE:
Bold, bright colours that help her stand out in a sea of monsters.

FREAKY FLAW:
She's a control shriek who needs to feel in charge of her unlife.

BFFs: Peri and Pearl Serpentine

Spiked hoop earrings resemble sea anemones

High-collared wrap with kraken pattern

Pink sea urchin bracelet

Orange fishbone arm cuff

Fluorescent yellow tentacles

"I deserved every single reward and trophy on the walls and shelves. No fish can deny I'm the beast dancer in the Great Scarrier Reef – probably in all of the seas."

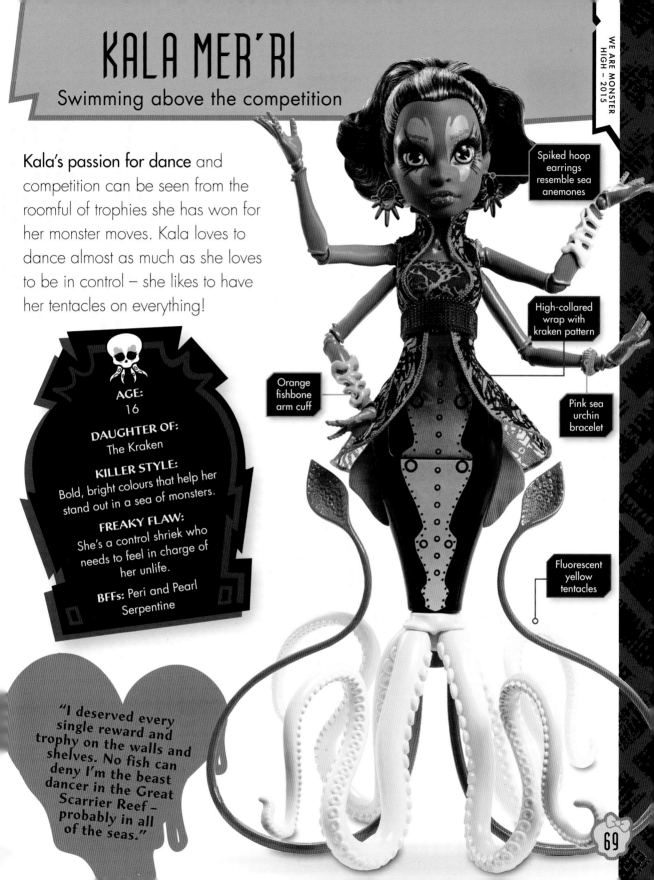

69

POSEA REEF
An ocean of knowledge

Black sand and coral headpiece

Blue coral earrings

Sleeveless tunic with aquatic print

Kelp arm wrap

Fishbone decoration

Pink coral body piece

Crab decoration

Green kelp skirt

Posea may be the daughter of Poseidon, the God of the Sea, but she's technically still a "goddess in training". Part of that training includes tending a garden of aquatic plants. Each plant represents a different sea creature, and Posea can tell how a sea creature is faring just by observing their plant!

AGE:
17

DAUGHTER OF: Poseidon

KILLER STYLE:
Flowing fabrics that swirl and sway like the ocean.

FREAKY FLAW:
Although she has a lot of knowledge in her head, Posea can't always fish it out!

BFFs: Peri and Pearl Serpentine

FREAKY FACT
The creatures in the kelp surrounding Posea glow in the dark.

PERI AND PEARL SERPENTINE
Of two minds about everything

Peri

Pearl

Peri and Pearl are sisters who are so close, they're literally inseparable! Of course, being so close doesn't mean that they always agree on everything, but they've learnt that working together gets them where they want to be much faster than trying to go their own way.

"The worst part about being a hydra with a twin is, if you are frighting, there is nowhere you can go to get away from each other."
– Peri

AGE:
16

DAUGHTERS OF:
The Hydra

KILLER STYLE: They're always looking for new ways to accessorise. "Double the baubles is twice as nice" is their motto

FREAKY FLAW: They constantly butt heads and don't always see eye-to-eye, but they literally always have each other's back.

BFFs: Kala Mer'ri and each other

Gold pirate-treasure-themed belt

Purple wing-fin

Single serpent tail

Pearl-and-jewel tail chains

71

STARS OF THE SILVER SCREAM

The ghouls and mansters of Monster High have starred in many movie adventures. Whether they join a roller-derby team or face a fishy transformation, they always have a scary-good time with their friends.

FRANKIE STEIN
Frankenstein's Halloween bride

Upswept Frankenstein's bride hair

Threaded nut earrings

Lightning-bolt masquerade mask

Welded metal arm cuffs

Oversized Skullette ring

Chainmail dress

Mesh overskirt with lightning bolts

Black, knee-high platform boots

Frankie is excited about Halloween until she finds out it's the one night of the year monsters stay inside! Determined to make it a celebration both for monsters and normies – from a neighbouring high school – alike, Frankie wears an outfit that pays tribute to her monster scaritage.

Halloween screening
Every year before Halloween, Mr Rotter shows his class an old black and white film warning them about the dangers of the holiday.

Boo goo
Frankie carries around this metallic cauldren when she goes trick-or-treating. It's overflowing with bootiful green goo.

74

CLAWDEEN WOLF
Werewolf gone wilder

Clawdeen joins Frankie in celebrating Halloween with a costume that howls about her werewolf bloodline. In the midst of all the Halloween happenings, Clawdeen reveals she has never been on a date – a situation that Draculaura is desperate to "help" with!

Purple-and-black-spotted shaved head

Gold and blue werewolf mask

Gold chest plate

Faux-fur sleeves are part of her jumpsuit

Purple mesh-patterned jumpsuit

Black, faux-fur leg warmers

Gold platform heels

Treats to die for
Clawdeen carries this coffin-shaped sweet box, stuffed to the brim with ghoulishous green treats.

"Gee, a double date with you, my brother, and some guy I've never met. How could a ghoul pass that up?"

FREAKY FACT
Draculaura sets up a round of speed dating for Clawdeen, but it is not a howling success.

75

DRACULAURA
Monster matchmaker

Spider-web eyelashes

Translucent bat mask

Red bat collar

Draculaura looks fangtastic for Halloween as a vamped-up vampire. She spends the holiday trying to give her beast friend Clawdeen the ultimate Halloween goodie – her first date! But from Clawdeen's point of view, it's more trick than treat.

Skeletonised purple-and-black bat wings

FREAKY FACT
Draculaura's birthday is February 14, Valentine's Day.

Leggings fade from pink to black

Party games
To keep the normies at the Halloween party, Draculaura brings a spookerific game – pin the bow on the Skullette skeleton!

White-and-purple dress with sheer train

Transparent ankle boots with fang heels

CLEO DE NILE
Princess with problems

Black hair with Nile blue streaks

Golden serpent necklace

Golden bandage mask

Blue-and-gold sheath dress

Black and metallic blue fishtail skirt

Blue and gold pyramid wedges

Even though she is dressed as the jewel of the Nile in honour of her royal Egyptian heritage, Cleo is less concerned with Halloween than the pressure she's under from her father and sister Nefera to break up with "that commoner", her boyfriend Deuce.

Drink like an Egyptian
Appropriately for an Egyptian princess, Cleo's Halloween party accessories are decorated with all things Egyptian – like her punch bowl with serpent ladle and Skullette cup.

FREAKY FACT
Cleo and Lilith, the queen bee from the neighbouring normie school, bond over fashion.

77

ABBEY BOMINABLE
Courageous yeti

Fur hat with ice crystal

Ice-crystal shoulder cover

Purple ice trick-or-treat basket

Ice mask

Belt looks like shards of ice

Shimmering sleeves with fur cuffs

Snowflake-patterned skirt

Ice-crystal high heels

Abbey dresses to express her yeti history for Halloween. When she protects Heath Burns from being pelted by a normie pumpkin trap at the dance, Heath can't get over being saved by a ghoul. He spends the night trying to save her from dangers more imagined than real.

Monster plan
Abbey and Operetta devise a plan to "drop" a chandelier on Abbey, so that Heath can rescue her.

Sweet treats
Abbey's treat for the party is suitably sweet and scary. The icing on the cake is a dapper spider wearing a top hat!

DRACULAURA
Birthday ghoul

Draculaura is getting ready for her Sweet 1600th Birthday! There's a party to plan and her driving test to study for. And if all that isn't enough, Kieran Valentine, an old boyfriend from her past, shows up and threatens to steal her heart… literally.

Pink bat-and-heart headband

Glittery pink hair

Lips with fangs handbag

Party dress in Draculaura's signature colours

Lace-frilled skirt with pink bows

Pink, cake-themed heels with black icing

"You know what, Valentine? It's time everyone knew how much your love stinks."

FREAKY FACT
Draculaura has a special three-tiered chocolate cake with pink icing made for her birthday.

Behind the wheel
What could be a better gift for your Sweet 1600th birthday than a scary-cool convertible roadster? This ride is made for Draculaura.

CLAWD WOLF
Sweet 1600th sweetheart

Blue-streaked fauxhawk

Patterned tuxedo jacket

Black shirt with teal tie

Coffin jewellery box and Sweet 1600 necklace

Grey-lens sunglasses

Grey jeans with yellow stitching

Polished, zip-up ankle boots

All suited up for Draculaura's Sweet 1600th birthday, Clawd thought nothing about the celebrations could be more difficult than finding the perfect gift for his boo love. Little did Clawd know he'd also be battling for Draculaura's heart with another monster suitor named Valentine.

Perfect present
After some guidance from Clawdeen, Clawd gets Draculaura this clawesome dress with a pink bow for her birthday.

Love test
Clawd also gives Draculaura the gift of a study guide for her driving test. Draculaura is less than thrilled, and Clawdeen taps Clawd's nose with a rolled up newspaper!

CLAWDEEN WOLF
Party planner

As her beast friend, Clawdeen is responsible for planning Draculaura's Sweet 1600th birthday party, but at least Draculaura's made it easy for Clawdeen – all she wants is everything! Clawdeen looks every inch the glamorous party planner for the event of the millennium.

Purple-glitter-streaked hair

Blue studded gloves

Purple bow tie

Black bolero with faux-fur cuffs

Gold tuxedo handbag

Cummerbund with moon adornment

Leopard-spot, three-quarter trousers

Buckled boots with spiked wedge heels

FREAKY FACT
As Clawd's sister, Clawdeen is concerned about Draculaura fanging out with her ex, Valentine.

Key to the party
Each of the guests at Draculaura's Sweet 1600th party has a Skullette skeleton key invite in a colour that matches their party outfit.

81

FRANKIE STEIN
Frankie to the rescue!

Silver
tinsel in
her hair

When a party-ready Frankie finds out that
Draculaura's ex-boyfriend, Valentine, plans
on stealing Draculaura's heart at her
Sweet 1600th, Frankie
charges into action. Seeking
advice from C.A. Cupid –
a ghoul who knows all about
love – Frankie comes up with
a plan to stop Valentine.

Black-and-
silver stitch,
mismatched
earrings

Black
bracelets with
silver stitches

*"Fantasies are great.
Reality can be
a bolt in
the neck
sometimes."*

Silver
lightning-
bolt purse

One-shouldered,
black-and-blue
tartan party dress

Heart-stopping mission
Frankie and C.A. Cupid track down Valentine
and use Cupid's arrow to stop him from
adding Draculaura's heart to his collection.

Black-and-blue
patchwork
pattern shoes

Black beanie cap

Right ear is always bent forwards

Pink hair with fringe

Blue vinyl jacket

Studded waist belt

Black dress with wolf prints

Chain-strap handbag with zip design

Pink leggings match her hair

Lace-up boots with gold spike tops

"Hey! It's my genie, not yours. And you can't tell me how to use my wishes!"

HOWLEEN WOLF
Be careful what you wish for...

When Howleen finds a magic lantern in the attic at Monster High and unleashes its genie, Gigi Grant, she is granted 13 wishes. Howleen sets out to make unlife better for her classmates – but an evil force has other plans!

FREAKY FACT

Howleen loves changing her look and isn't afraid to try new styles – like these long pink locks!

Greedy genie
Howleen unleashes Gigi's evil shadow form, Whisp, too. Whisp plays on Howleen's desire to be popular to influence what she wishes for, and attempts to take over the world!

LAGOONA BLUE
Freshwater monster mode

Lagoona and Gil love each other, but Gil's parents don't love that Lagoona is a saltwater monster. This causes Lagoona and Gil much heartache. When Howleen transforms Lagoona into a freshwater monster, it looks like all their problems are solved. That is, until Lagoona starts acting fishy.

Freshwater breathing mask

Green turtle necklace matches bracelet

One-piece swimdress

Fishbowl handbag

Mesh cover-up

Wedge sandals with weed details

"Gil's parents are going to flip their fins when they see me!"

Aquatic accessories
Lagoona has brightened up her new freshwater look by putting a vivid pink flower in her hair.

FREAKY FACT
Gil is not happy that Lagoona is now a freshwater monster – he thinks she was perfect before.

84

DRACULAURA
A shadow of her former self

Draculaura finds that running afoul of Howleen's wishes gets her transported inside Gigi's lantern and replaced by an evil shadow form of herself. At least Draculaura isn't alone, as Howleen eventually sends the rest of the ghouls there as well!

Gold bat-wing crown

Gold-tinsel-streaked hair

Gold bat-wing necklace

FREAKY FACT
Draculaura's heart-shaped birthmark is gold instead of red.

Lost in a lantern
Howleen's wish leads to Draculaura being held inside this translucent pink genie lantern.

Dressed to thrill
The back of Draculaura's dress features a stylised bat-wing, cobweb and Skullette design.

Lace-layered asymmetric skirt

Gold-and-pink webbed slipper wedges

FRANKIE STEIN
Haunt the Kasbah

Frankie may be the nicest ghoul at school, but that doesn't stop Howleen from wishing her away from Monster High. Reunited with her other beasties inside Gigi's lantern, Frankie and the ghouls discover a way to stop Whisp, the shadow genie, from taking over the world.

Gold nut crown

Gold nut earrings

Blue hair with gold tinsel

Gold lightning chest plate

Silver, black and blue halterneck dress

Holding gold
Frankie's neck, arm and leg stitches are coloured gold rather than silver.

Magic mirror
Frankie and the ghouls find a magic mirror that has the power to stop Whisp's evil plan.

Gold, lightning-strike skirt details

Gold wedge sandals with blue straps

CLAWDEEN WOLF
Wished-away sister

Clawdeen is not exactly pleased with the way Howleen uses her newfound wishes, and is afraid her little sister is making some big mistakes. Howleen, on the other hand, is not exactly pleased about her older sister telling her what to do – so she wishes Clawdeen into Gigi's lantern, too!

FREAKY FACT

The Clawdeen, Frankie and Draculaura 13 Wishes dolls all come with their own genie lamp to match their outfit.

Genie details
Clawdeen's gold accessories, like this winding zip bangle, add to her genie-inspired look.

"Jealous? Everybody's right about these wishes, they've changed you."

Golden zip headdress

Gold-sparkle eye shadow

Gold-sparkle lipstick

Purple plait with gold tinsel

Black-and-gold dress with moon designs

Three-layered overskirt with gold zip pattern on top

Gold wedges with purple zip straps

FRANKIE STEIN
Black and white fright

Blunt bob, parted to the side

Frankie is unexpectedly spending spring break on Skull Shores. She is monstrously excited to discover that the island's Tiki monsters treat her like royalty. That is, until she finds herself being used as bait to lure a giant rampaging beast. She looks so frightened, she seems to have lost all her colour!

The Beast of Skull Shores
Frankie is terrified when a huge purple beast grabs her, but she soon realises that he means no harm.

Monokini with stormy sky patterns

Waist wrap has matching thunderstorm details

Cloud-grey sandals with stacked-nut heels

FREAKY FACT
This is the second Frankie doll created in eerie black and white. The first was her San Diego Comic Con 2010 exclusive (p.192).

A splash of colour
A full-colour Escape From Skull Shores Frankie doll was later released as part of a pack, along with Ghoulia, Cleo, Draculaura and Clawdeen.

ABBEY BOMINABLE

Spring-break snow queen

Abbey's first visit to the tropics is quite an adjustment from the cold she is used to. Not one to complain, she dresses in her most spooktacular swimsuit and makes the beast of things. Warmhearted Abbey even manages to win over the Tiki monsters to help rescue Frankie.

Ice crystal earrings

Large sunhat offers much-needed shade

Dish of pink shave ice

One-piece swimsuit with snowflake pattern

Skullette key bracelet

Cover-up has snowflake pattern, too

Ice-crystal high-heeled sandals

Ice getaway
Abbey escapes from a pit by freezing the Tiki monsters and climbing them like stairs.

Skull Shores
Abbey is prepared for her holiday with a detailed map of the area.

89

GHOULIA YELPS
Beach brainiac

Brain-shaped hair clip

Coconut cup with brain-freeze smoothie

Red-collared, buttoned-down swimsuit

Ghoulia has swapped her horn-rimmed glasses for shockingly cool sunglasses and is ready for spring break! Ghoulia regards any holiday as an opportunity to gain knowledge. She probably doesn't expect that to include learning how to negotiate help from Tiki monsters, though!

Genius accessories
One of Ghoulia's earrings is shaped like a lung and the other is shaped like a brain – which is fitting for the smartest ghoul in school!

Brain-patterned cover skirt

Petrifying performance
Ghoulia and Abbey enjoy the show put on by the island's residents... before it turns scary (and not in a good way!).

Blood-drop heeled sandal

CLEO DE NILE
Princess on holiday

Cleo, being royalty, always expects to be treated as such. When the ghouls arrive on Skull Shores, it comes as quite a shock to her when it is Frankie who receives the royal treatment and not her – especially when her gold make-up and matching swimsuit clearly have the royal touch.

"What is going on here? Why is Frankie getting the royal treatment? My treatment?!"

FREAKY FACT
This Cleo doll only appears in a pack with Ghoulia, Draculaura, Clawdeen and a full-colour Frankie.

Bobbed hairstyle with blue fringe

Gold lamé swimsuit – fit for a princess!

Egyptian-style cuff bracelet

Bandage and palm design on jumpsuit combine mummy chic with tropical style

Mummy's best friend
Cleo's cool beach sandals have a figure of a man with a dog's head for the heels. He is Anubis, the Egyptian god of mummification and the afterlife.

91

LAGOONA BLUE
Monster homecoming

Lagoona can't wait to spend spring break with her friends and manster on the Great Scarrier Reef, where she is from. She loves the beautiful water, ocean breeze and wearing her favourite beachwear. But she loves her manster, Gil, the most – especially when he overcomes his fear of saltwater to be a hero!

Tentacle and octopus mismatched earrings

Tank top with sheer frill

Algae smoothie in a Tiki cup

Beach comfort
Lagoona likes to be sporty on the beach, so she wears shorts under her wrap.

Pink fish-scale wrap

"You're gonna love The Great Scarrier Reef, Gil. It's the most beautiful place in the world."

Shoes from the deep
Lagoona's shoes look like they come from the ocean – just like Lagoona. They have a wave pattern and bubble design on the heels.

Transparent-blue sandals

ABBEY BOMINABLE
She's got monster skills

Abbey's more used to ice skating than roller skating, so the world of Skultimate Roller Maze (SKRM) is all new to her. The annual roller-derby tournament still seems odd to her, but she straps on her skates and joins the team to help her friends.

Sparkly igloo helmet

Colourful, glitter-streaked hair

Icicle choker necklace

Black mesh overshirt

Cracked-ice pattern on dress

Fur-lined skates with icicle heels

Solo skater
Glitter ghoul Abbey was first released in a set with Ghoulia. She was later released as a solo figure, without the glittery hair and with a darker helmet.

"I have been skating since I was knee high to yak."

93

FRANKIE STEIN
From fearleader to leader

When it looks like the Monster High SKRM team is going to fall apart because there aren't enough mansters to field a team, fearleader Frankie recruits a team of ghouls to take their place. What she lacks in knowledge about the game, she makes up for in determination.

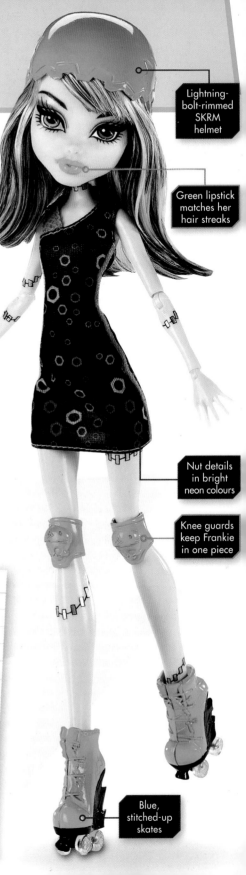

Lightning-bolt-rimmed SKRM helmet

Green lipstick matches her hair streaks

Nut details in bright neon colours

Knee guards keep Frankie in one piece

Blue, stitched-up skates

FREAKY FACT
Monster High battles against their arch rivals in the SKRM final showdown. They face the gargoyles from Granite City High.

"Okay, enough! Your school is crumbling around you and all you care about is stupid tradition?!"

Rallying school spirit
When the SKRM team loses their game, they forfeit their school crest and, with it, their school spirit – a phantom who guards the school. Frankie resolves to get them both back.

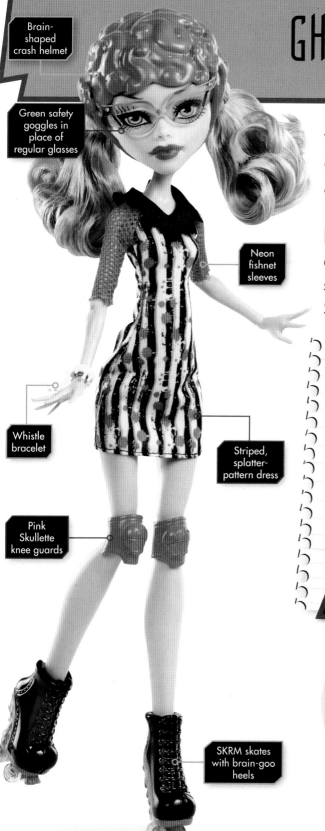

GHOULIA YELPS
Zooming zombie

- Brain-shaped crash helmet
- Green safety goggles in place of regular glasses
- Neon fishnet sleeves
- Whistle bracelet
- Striped, splatter-pattern dress
- Pink Skullette knee guards
- SKRM skates with brain-goo heels

There is no bigger SKRM fan than Ghoulia. She can rattle off the names of the greatest skaters in history, including their stats. It's Ghoulia's knowledge of this history, plus her own genius, that she calls upon when she finds and reassembles Robecca Steam, the greatest SKRM player ever.

Reassembling a hero
Ghoulia uses her scientific skills to rebuild Robecca Steam – a SKRM legend who was broken into pieces during a race a century ago.

"There are no rules against ghouls playing SKRM. In fact, perhaps the greatest player ever was a ghoul called Robecca Steam."*
*Translated from Zombie-speak

95

OPERETTA
Track record

Operetta learned to skate almost before she could walk. She has supreme confidence in her abilities and a fearless style that complements them. Operetta's independent streak kept her from joining the SKRM team – until she realised they really needed her help to win.

Trademark eye mask attaches to helmet

Green-streaked ponytail

There's no "I" in SKRM
Operetta normally avoids organised school sports, but soon gets in tune with the rest of the SKRM team.

White SKRM uniform with retro record graphics

Treble-clef-shaped heel

Safety first
Intricate and elegant musical-note patterns decorate Operetta's SKRM helmet, to combine fashion with function.

White, lace-up SKRM skates

LAGOONA BLUE
Smooth skater

Finned SKRM helmet

Angler fish and piranha print top

Natural fins help Lagoona glide along the track

Aqua-green knee guards

SKRM skates have bubble laces

Lagoona is a huge fan of SKRM and shows up at every match to cheer for the Monster High team. When Frankie asks for volunteers to be a part of an all-ghouls team, Lagoona jumps at the chance to get in the maze and skate for Monster High.

"Skatin' ain't about strength, mates. It's about balance and coordination. It's like glidin' in the water."

FREAKY FACT
Lagoona's right hand is making the "shaka" sign. This is often used by surfers to mean "hang loose", or relax.

Streamlined shoes
Aerodynamic fins on the back of her skates allow Lagoona to speed past her rivals.

97

CLAWDEEN WOLF
Knocking spots off the competition

Helmet has spikes, spots and ear holes

Purple ponytail with green streaks

Neon-green fishnet sleeve

Leopard-print SKRM uniform

Racing-stripe design

Protective Skullette knee guards

Spiky SKRM skates

Clawdeen's natural werewolf strength and speed make her a formidable skater. Some mansters think SKRM isn't a sport "for ghouls", but growing up with lots of older brothers helped prepare Clawdeen for the rough-and-tumble action on the SKRM track.

"I was dragged to every game Clawd played...so I learned everything about it, whether I wanted to or not."

Team player
During the game, Clawdeen gives up her place on the SKRM team so that Draculaura gets a chance to play.

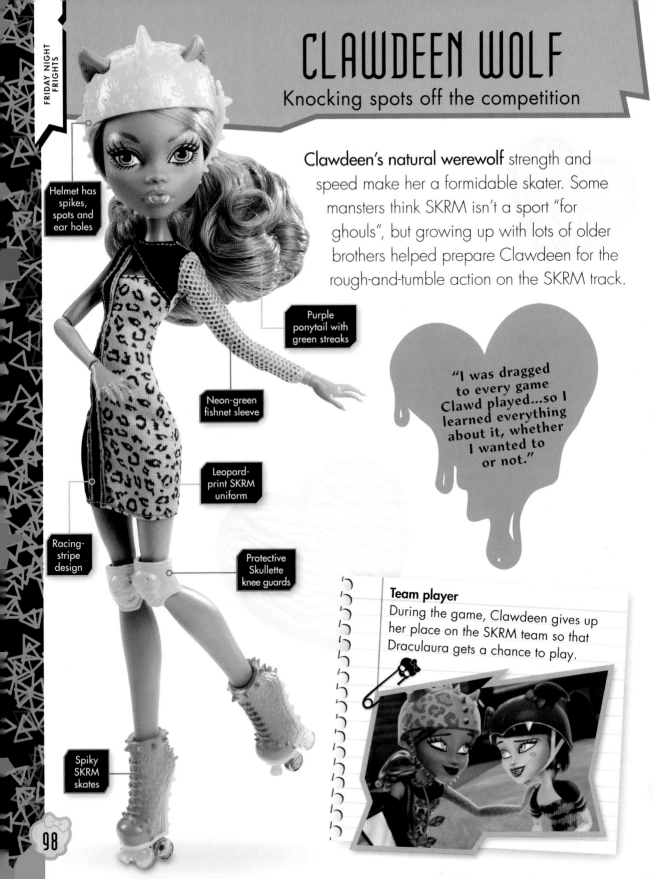

DRACULAURA
Temporary vampire queen

Draculaura has been proclaimed the Queen of the Vampires! She's thrilled… until she finds out it's not true. Draculaura and her friends discover that the real queen is a famous actress. The star invites the ghouls to her boovie premiere and coronation in Hauntlywood!

Black beaded earrings match necklace

Black-carpet fashion – beaded dress with bat design

Pink, dripping vampire-lips purse

Pearl chain and bat charm belt

Bat-wing-shaped hem

"I can't be Queen. It would mean leaving all of my friends, and Monster High is my home."

FREAKY FACT
The Vampire's Heart, a magical artifact that glows in the presence of royalty, doesn't glow for Draculaura. She knows then that she can't be the real queen.

Black-carpet shoes
Draculaura's spooktacular shoes for the boovie premiere are draped with pearls, and feature bat, heart and lips charms.

The Vampire's Heart motif

99

LAGOONA BLUE
Sea-sational sense of style

Lagoona may prefer fanging out in tank tops, board shorts and flip-flops, but that doesn't mean she can't dive into the diva look if she wants to. When the opportunity to go to Hauntlywood rolls in, Lagoona makes waves on the black carpet.

Pearl headband with a mollusk design

Black pearl necklace

Coral-and-blue, bead-textured dress

Black jellyfish purse

Horror show
Lagoona and Gil walk the black carpet for the premiere of the new Vampire Majesty movie.

Shoe-stoppers
Lagoona's pearly pink heeled sandals have shell charms and a single black pearl on the front.

CLEO DE NILE
A look to die for

Cleo may not be an actress, but as an Ancient Egyptian princess she's well acquainted with drama. Even though the Hauntlywood black carpet hasn't been rolled out just for Cleo, she walks it like boovie-star royalty.

"I mean, being a fake queen is still better than not being royal at all."

Green gem on cheek – it is usually blue

Gold Egyptian charm belt

Bead-textured wrap dress with sheer, sparkling hem

Gold scarab handbag

Gold heels with serpent straps

Regal tiara
Cleo's Egyptian headband has a scarab beetle on one side and a serpent on the other.

101

CLAWDEEN WOLF
Fierce fashionista

Clawdeen is always there for her ghouls – even if it means taking a trip around the world. She joins her big sister Clawdia in Londoom to help solve the mystery of the Queen of the Vampires. She doesn't expect the adventure to take her to the black carpet in Hauntlywood!

"Hauntlywood, get ready to meet Monster High!"

Gold moon ear cuff

Purple, moon-shaped handbag

Gold belt with chains and moon charms

Black-carpet dress has clawesome ruffled trim

Gold heels with cut-outs and stud, chain and pearl details

A friend indeed
At the premiere, ever-helpful Clawdeen gives Draculaura a whistle. She blows it and is reunited with her manster, Clawd.

LAGOONAFIRE
Lagoona Blue fused with Jinafire Long

When a time-machine accident fuses Lagoona, a sea monster, with Jinafire, a fiery Chinese dragon, there's bound to be steam. The resulting Lagoonafire fusion blows both hot and cold, but she eventually finds balance in the blending of the two ghouls' polar-opposite talents.

Hair rolled into waves and pinned back with pink coral beads

Webbed fingers

Pink jellyfish handbag has tentacles

Pale blue dragon tail

"A good swim is just what we need to let off a little steam!"

In hot water
Perhaps a dip in the Monster High pool was not the best idea for Lagoonafire. She ends up turning its water into steam!

Coral strappy shoes with wave-shaped heel

Sea dragon
Lagoonafire has fishy fins but also a fiery dragon's tail and scales. Watch out for her new fire-breathing skills, too!

Steampunk goggles with heart-shaped lenses

DRACUBECCA
Draculaura fused with Robecca Steam

Mechanical bat wings

Umbrella handle with bat detail

Copper cage skirt with heart and bat detail

Black frill edge to heart-print and striped dress

Steam-powered rocket boots with pink thrusters

Draculaura and Robecca are both kind and considerate, but when an accident fuses them together, Dracubecca finds herself spending more time apologising than getting used to her new body! It takes teamwork and coordination for the ghouls to take charge of their new (con)fusion.

"It's like, my brain tells me to do one thing but something inside makes me do something else."

FREAKY FACT
Unlike Draculaura, Dracubecca can walk in the sun without an umbrella. She carries one out of habit (and to match her outfit!).

Stage fright
The fusing of monster and machine-monster is an explosive combination. While rehearsing for the school play, Dracubecca's rocket boots make her crash-land stage left.

CLEOLEI
Cleo de Nile fused with Toralei

Gold headband adorned with purrfect cat charm

Shimmering bolero jacket with bow collar

Turquoise belt with central cat buckle

Egyptian cat-print jumpsuit

Golden handbag with cat motif

These two fused ghouls would rather be stuck with anyone but each other! When Toralei's catlike curiosity causes Cleo and Toralei to combine, the resulting Cleolei finds herself clawing at her mummy wrappings to escape the situation. Only by working together can Cleolei land on her feet.

Copycat
Not wanting to miss out, Scarah Screams gets in on the freaky action by dressing up as Toralei! Scarah's fake Toralei-style claws, cat's tail, pointed ears and cattish handbag are all in response to the fusion events.

"I am still the queen of this body! You're just visiting!"
—Cleo, to Toralei

Claws out
Cleolei manages to strike a balance between fine feline accessories and golden touches fit for a princess with this glove, worn on one hand.

Wedges with studded straps and cat-eye toes

105

Wolf-like ears have leaf details

CLAWVENUS
Clawdeen Wolf fused with Venus McFlytrap

Faux-fur, two-tone shrug

Clawvenus is a fusion of two friends who couldn't be more different. At first, Clawdeen's strong personality and werewolf senses have a hard time mixing with Venus's laid-back environmentalism and pollen powers, but the two find a balance and bring out the best in each other through meditation.

Leopard print and mesh top

Gold creeping-vine bangle

Skirt with a vibrant green pollen print

Tangled up
Clawvenus's style is vine-tastic. Even her handbag is crawling with woven flora detail, and is coloured a fresh lime green to match.

FREAKY FACT
Clawdeen has plant allergies. She does not cope well with this flora-filled fusion!

Pink vines encircle black heeled shoes

Placard protest
To show their solidarity with Frankie after she sacrifices herself to unfuse them, her ghoulfriends rally together to support her. Clawdeen wears a "Save Frankie" T-shirt and carries a placard.

FRANKIE STEIN
Fearless friend

Blue hair with black and yellow streaks

Blue, bolt-patterned stitches

Bolt-cut neckline

Metal belt with chain detail

Lightning-bolt charms also attach to recharge chamber

Electric-energy-print dress

Yellow lightning-bolt heels

When her friends are fused together, Frankie makes the ultimate sacrifice to free them. She uses the power of her own life-force to unfuse her friends, but she is left without her own, causing her to collapse. Luckily, her friends find a way to return Frankie's spark – and she gets a shocking new look in the process!

FREAKY FACT

Frankie later dresses as Clawdeen Wolf – from her curly hair to her clawed fingers – in response to the fusion events.

"You took my friends from me! The ones that I LOVE!"

Save Frankie!
After sacrificing herself to save her friends, Frankie needs to recharge herself in this coffin-shaped recharge chamber. It literally is a hair-raising experience for Frankie!

DRACULAURA
Haunted ghoul

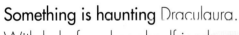

Something is haunting Draculaura. With help from her ghoulfriends and a juicy lead from journalist Spectra, Draculaura sets out to find out just who (or what) has been haunting her. The answer takes her much further than she could have imagined and deep into the ghost world, where she herself gets a ghostly look.

FREAKY FACT

The entrance to the ghost world is revealed when the ghouls follow Spectra up to the Monster High attic!

Skin has an iridescent, ghostly hue

Pink-and-black swept-back hair

Silver, bat-shaped collar necklace

Cloak forms billowing bat wings

Miniature silver bats and hearts form links to chains

See-through shoes have chain details

Haunted happenings
There is something odd going on at Monster High – lockers open by themselves and carrots float in midair. Worst of all, the haunting makes Draculaura's hair stand up on end!

SPECTRA VONDERGEIST
Spirit with a story

Bootifully styled purple hair

Detention chain corset

Floaty dress with jagged hem

Locks hang from Spectra's chains

Silver chains and locks to her knees

Spectra's love for sensational journalism can sometimes get her into trouble. An investigation into the haunting at Monster High leads Spectra to the ghost world where friends, old and new, are in need of her help. She breathes life back into her old school – Haunted High – where ghosts are being chained up for crimes they didn't commit.

Gruesome twosome
When she runs into trouble at Haunted High, Spectra is pleased to receive help from Porter "Paintergeist" Geiss. The duo work together to end the hauntings at Monster High.

"Okay ghouls, who's got a story? I've got the need for leads. Gimme the gossip! What's the scoop?"

FREAKY FACT

The detention chains from Haunted High don't work on "solid" ghouls, but can ensnare Spectra because she is a ghost!

109

TWYLA
Boogey frights

Black bow headband

Ghostly blue eyeshadow

Being the daughter of the Boogeyman means Twyla has some tricks up her sleeves. Borrowing her father's Boogey Sand lets her turn her friends into ghosts and back again, allowing them to travel to the ghost world – and to Haunted High. For a monster who walks the line between "solid" and ghost, Twyla is particularly suited for an adventure to the other side.

Boogey Sand held within hourglass charm on bracelet

Milky skin tone brought on by using Boogey Sands

Ectoplasm goo heels

FREAKY FACT
All of the Haunted-themed dolls have a luminous, milky hue to their skin.

"You ghouls ready to get ghosty?"

Boogey-Sand bracelet
Twyla can take Boogey Sand with her into the ghost world, stashed within this bracelet. Each of the Haunted ghouls (except for Spectra, who is already a ghost) wears one of these.

CLAWDEEN WOLF
Ghost hunter

Clawdeen is the best friend a ghoul could have. Even after Spectra started a rumour that she had were-fleas, Clawdeen never hesitated to help her solve the hauntings and right the wrongs happening at Spectra's old school, Haunted High. Forgiveness and loyalty make Clawdeen the ghoul to have in your corner when things get ghostly.

Scare-brush
Ghostly times call for ghostly accessories. This hairbrush might be see-through, but it can still create hairstyles to be seen dead in.

"I promised Spectra I'd help her find a story. And whatever she's after, I'm not letting her go alone."

Multi-chain waist belt

Moon-pattern dress with sheer tulle

Crescent moon on chains

Gold-chain sandal boots with a half-moon heel

CLAWDEEN WOLF
Crystal Comet partygoer

The lights of Boo York are calling Clawdeen, and she can't wait to hit the city! When Cleo invites her to join her family for the arrival of the mysterious Crystal Comet, Clawdeen knows she'll have to dress to impress. Her love of fashion makes her feel right at home shopping and taking in the best Boo York has to offer.

"Oh my ghoul look at this view! I think I can see Boo Jersey from here."

I heart Boo York
For frightseeing, Clawdeen decides to make an impact! She chooses this chic graffiti top spelling out her "Love" for Boo York city.

Golden crystal shades

Ripped waistcoat

Gold-thread shorts

Handbag with claw clasp

Studded, heeled trainers

112

DRACULAURA
Frightseeing fashionista

Draculaura will never turn down the chance to take a trip with her ghoulfriends, and she has been saving her urban style for a big city break. Boo York has enough sights to keep them busy for weeks, but the ghouls have to cram in as much sightseeing as they can before the gala – and the comet – arrives.

The letter "D" decorates her dress, along with hearts and fangs

City skyline cut to edge of shiny silver skirt

Lip-shaped handbag has vampire fangs

Grey gargoyle shoe-boots

FREAKY FACT
Draculaura changes into a ballgown for the Crystal Comet party.

Sharp shades
Draculaura can shield her eyes from the glare of shiny city skyscrapers (or passing comets) with these sunglasses. Now she looks just the part for frightseeing.

113

OPERETTA
Music monstro

There's nowhere like Boo York to take in music from around the world. Operetta has dreamed of the street-corner musicians and Bloodway greats alike, and the chance to hear it all is music to her ears. First, though, she wants to make sure that she looks the part of a Bloodway belle!

Purple crystal shades

Red vinyl T-shirt top

Graffiti-inspired print

Spider-web handbag

Iridescent purple, lace-up boots

Shades and shards
Like Clawdeen and Draculaura, Operetta sports a stylish pair of crystal shades to the Crystal Comet party.

"Toldja we'd hear some scary-fun street music!"

FREAKY FACT
Operetta's hypnotic abilities mean she can't ever sing to a live audience!

114

NEFERA DE NILE
Scheming sibling

Nefera has one goal in mind: to be the best. Whether that's for herself or her family, nothing matters but the win. When the coming of the Crystal Comet to Boo York offers the chance to bind the De Niles to a powerful Egyptian family, Nefera tries to break up her sister Cleo and Deuce to secure her own family's wealth with a marriage.

Crystal Comet shard

Fierce bronze warrior armour

Serpent and crystal earrings

Twisted turquoise pattern adorns dress

Mark of the pharoahs
Nefera has a birthmark on her left shoulder that she often keeps covered because she is self-conscious of it.

Double-crossing sister
Nefera loves and craves power. She'll stop at nothing to get it regardless of what she has to do or who she might need to betray – including her own sister Cleo.

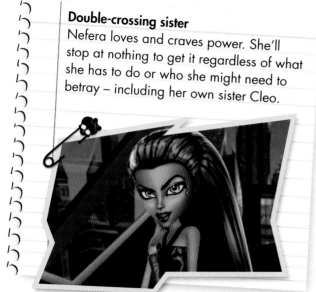

Serpentine gladiator sandals

FREAKY FACT
As part of her nefarious plan, Nefera uses a Crystal Comet shard to steal people's voices!

CATTY NOIR
Star of Boo York

Crystalised cat-ear headband

Crystal epaulettes cover a shimmering pink dress

Pink fingerless "opera-style" gloves

Cat-shaped handbag on wrist

Strappy heels with crystalline ankle straps

Even when she was a successful pop star, Catty never felt like she knew her true voice. Singing other people's songs left her feeling empty and confused. She follows Cleo to Boo York in search of her own sound and finds that music, like love, can be found in unexpected places, and sometimes the best songs are sung in harmony.

FREAKY FACT
While on a break from touring, Catty has been working on developing her own lyrical style.

"They offered me fame – money – they wanted to make me the pop queen of the world – and I gave it all up to try and find what you have."

Boo yeah
In Boo York, Catty finds herself mixing things up and duetting with rapper Seth Ptolemy, a.k.a. Pharaoh. This experience helps her end her writer's block.

LAGOONA BLUE
A fishy tale

Lagoona's secret stage fright leads to her embarrassing herself in front of the whole school, an unexpected trip home to the Great Scarrier Reef, and a fishtastic transformation. Facing her fears helps Lagoona see that there are worse things in unlife than trying and failing, especially when those you love are there to support you.

"That's ancient fishtory. I don't dance anymore."

Kraken chaos
When the ghouls face a huge monster known as the Kraken, Lagoona finds herself on the receiving end of a grip so strong it can only be broken by the truth.

Ponytail with teal and magenta stripes

Blue swim top

Flower necklace with beads

Glow-in-the-dark wings

Scaly fish's tail

Elaborate tail fins

TORALEI
Lionfish who learns her lesson

Kelp necklace

Lionfish fin rays

Stripes glow in the dark

Multiple lionfish tail fins

"I've been fishified... it's my worst nightmare!"

Toralei never predicted that a simple prank would end so badly. She only meant to embarrass Lagoona, not get all of the ghouls sucked down to the Great Scarrier Reef and turned into sea creatures! Now, helping Lagoona face her fears is the only way for Torelei to get them all home and make up for what she's done.

Pool party peril
Even though Toralei uses Lagoona's stage fright to make fun of her, when Toralei falls into a pool, Lagoona doesn't hestitate to leap in and save her.

FREAKY FACT
It is Posea Reef, the guardian of the reef, who transforms Toralei into a lionfish. Lionfish are beautiful predators with long, spiked fins that have poisonous tips.

DRACULAURA
Vampire of the deep

Draculaura is no stranger to changing shape. Her bat form is an easy way to get between classes and see over crowds. Being turned into a fish, on the other hand, takes some getting used to. Once she has her sea-fins her new ability to squeeze under rocks and through small spaces makes navigating the ocean a breeze.

Yellow tentacle necklace

Yellow glow-in-the-dark wings

Tentacle-shaped bangle

Torso decorated with dots and bats

Tentacles with black spikes underneath

"Check it out ghouls... clawesome, right?"

FREAKY FACT

Fittingly, the marine animal Posea Reef transforms Draculaura into is a vampire squid. The two have something in common – neither the vampire squid nor Draculaura actually drink blood!

Squid shading
The tentacle patterns around Draculaura's eyes are accented with shimmering dots, which recall the suckers on a squid's tentacles.

CLAWDEEN WOLF
Fierce wolffish

Teal and purple highlights

Purple skin like a wolffish

Glow-in-the-dark pectoral fins

Body chain with moon pendants

Clawdeen knows that being a good friend sometimes means letting someone figure things out for themselves. She'll never turn down the chance to support Lagoona when she needs it, but this sea wolf knows when to step up and when to stand down. Under the sea, her friendship and understanding are every bit as important as her new camouflage skills.

"A word of advice to all you ghouls out there: if you're ever thinking about looking a Kraken in the eye – don't."

Hooked on style
Clawdeen's new earring is copper-coloured, and shaped like a fish hook.

Tail decorated with crescent moons

Clawdeen stands independently on her tail fins

FREAKY FACT
This is the second doll that shows Clawdeen in a form that is not full werewolf. The first was her Freaky Fusion doll in which she was fused with Venus to make Clawvenus.

120

FRANKIE STEIN
Shockingly stylish

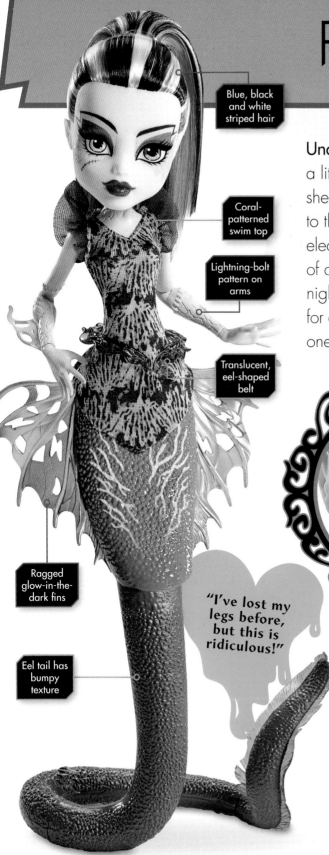

Blue, black and white striped hair

Coral-patterned swim top

Lightning-bolt pattern on arms

Translucent, eel-shaped belt

Ragged glow-in-the-dark fins

Eel tail has bumpy texture

"I've lost my legs before, but this is ridiculous!"

Underwater activities have always been a little bit shocking for Frankie. But when she and her ghoulfriends get transported to the Great Scarrier Reef, things get electrifying. With the powers and the tail of an electric eel, Frankie can light up the night and keep the sea monsters away... for a while. But it will take more than one ghoul to take on the Kraken.

Bolt from the blue
Frankie's eye make-up and eyebrows zigzag into a stylish lightning-bolt shape. Smaller yellow lightning bolts and blue dots, like the markings of a tropical fish, decorate her cheekbones.

FREAKY FACT
Normally electric eels are freshwater creatures, but it seems that Posea Reef, daughter of the God of the Seas, Poseidon, is allowed to bend the rules!

121

EYECONIC COLLECTIONS

The **world of Monster High** is full of bizarre happenings. Luckily the ghouls have an outfit for every odd occasion, from cosy creepovers to sticky-sweet situations. They even discover new Power Ghoul identities!

LITTLE DEAD RIDING WOLF

Once upon a time...there was a ghoul with a nose for trouble

Red-streaked hair

Clawdeen gets a chance to be fashionably old fashioned for a jaunt to granwolf's house as Little Dead Riding Wolf. On the way, she encounters a fiery ne'er-boo-well with his eyes on the goodies in Little Dead's picnic casket.

Lace-up bodice dress with strap decoration

Purple picnic casket

"I'm headed to granwolf's with this casket of cheer, and there's a full moon in the sky, so I have nothing to fear."

Red hood with animal print inside

Basket-weave platform boots

Custom hood
Little Dead Riding Wolf's red cape has holes on either side for Clawdeen's pointy ears to fit through.

SNOW BITE

Once upon a time... there was a ghoul whose beauty reflected her heart

Draculaura takes a turn as Snow Bite, a scary-tale ghoul with little use for mirrors – magical or otherwise. In another part of the kingdom lives a royal ghoul, who takes everything at face value. She's not happy that Snow Bite is considered more beautiful than her.

FREAKY FACT

Cleo de Nile makes an appearance as the royal ghoul, who refuses to be next in line to any other ghoul's beauty.

"You see my face is not reflected in polished metal, still water or glass..."

Skullette apple hair piece

Bow with pink apple pattern

Green drip dress

Dripping apple handbag

Green apple heels

Scary-tale storybook

Each of the Scarily Ever After dolls comes with a booklet that tells the story of their scary-tale character. In Snow Bite's, the royal ghoul creates a cursed apple that will make Snow Bite the "fairest no more".

125

THREADARELLA
Once upon a time... there was a ghoul who wished for more

Frankie has taken on the role of a famous scary-tale character who is forced by her three catty were-sisters to sew clothes all day. Threadarella longs for a freaky fabulous unlife. Then with the help of her fairy ghoulmother, she finally gets her scarily ever after.

Crown of needles, pins and thread

Pin earrings

Thread reel handbag

Multi-fabric ballgown

Heels laced up with thread

Forgotten foot
When the clock strikes midnight, Threadarella is in such a hurry to get away that she runs from the ball leaving not only her shoe, but her foot as well!

"It's been great but it's really late and now it's time I flew!"

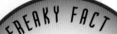
FREAKY FACT
Toralei, Meowlody and Purrsephone appear as Frankie's were-sisters, Abbey Bominable as the fairy ghoulmother and Jackson/Holt as the prince.

Cutting edge
The high heels on Threadarella's shoes are silver scissors.

WONDER WOLF
A howling force for justice

Studded headband

Metallic bodysuit with upturned green collar

Purple cuff bracelet

Belt features different phases of the moon

Shorts with comic-book burst pattern

Shield with howling werewolf and phases of the moon

Platform boots with studs and spikes

Clawdeen hears a mysterious voice calling her into the catacombs where she finds a secret door. Behind it, Clawdeen discovers that she is heir to the powers of the super hero Wonder Wolf! Now, her clawesome abilities have been added to the Power Ghouls team.

FREAKY FACT

Wonder Wolf has extraordinary strength and speed, plus heightened senses – all three of which increase during a full moon. She can also throw her shield and have it return to her.

Wonder-ful read
A mini comic book comes packaged with the doll. The cover of *Wonder Wolf* Issue #1 shows her smashing through a solid brick wall.

Explosive earrings
As well as gold hoops, Wonder Wolf wears these spiky starburst earrings with werewolf Skullettes in the centre.

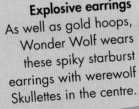

127

VOLTAGEOUS
Charging up the power of justice!

Power-bolt headband

Power-bolt earrings match headband

Lightning-bolt cape

When a lab accident gives Frankie extraordinary powers, she seeks out Ghoulia for help. Ghoulia reveals herself to be Ms Deadfast, leader of the Power Ghouls. She teaches Frankie to use her powers and gives her a name… Voltageous!

Electrifying story
In the first issue of her comic book, Voltageous draws on the power of justice to strike fear into the hearts of evildoers.

Removable wrap with comic-burst pattern

FREAKY FACT
Voltageous can drain the power from anything that stores or carries electricity. She can then fire that power in the form of lightning bolts or use it as magnetic force.

Striking jewellery
Voltageous wears shockingly cool accessories, including silver cuffs with lightning bolts.

"It's not like I planned on being a super hero."

Tall boots feature electrical coils and sparks

128

POLTERGHOUL
The justice that goes bump in the night

Spectra was once part of a secret society that guards a powerful artifact called the Collar of Chaos. When the collar is stolen, Spectra is summoned by a spirit and given new powers to retrieve the collar. She becomes Polterghoul!

Chain headband

Chain cape

Skullette earrings dangle on chains

Silver trim on dress matches belt

Ball-and-chain belt

Chain-wrapped boots

FREAKY FACT
Polterghoul can move things with her mind, pass through solid objects and cause her chains to extend out to grab and wrap up objects.

Polter-cool comic
The cover of Issue #1 shows Polterghoul passing through a wall, ready to bind evil with her chains of justice.

ISSUE 1

POLTERGHOUL

MARDIE · RILEY · JUAREZ · SANDER · SHIPMAN · YELPS

"I think I shall call myself... Polterghoul!"

Rattling chains
Polterghoul's ball-and-chain belt is secured with a padlock at the back – for now.

129

CAT TASTROPHE
Villain with cat-titude

No monster knows how Toralei really became Cat Tastrophe because she changes the story every time she tells it! What they do know is that she unlives to spread disorder and confusion – and that only the Power Ghouls can stop her.

Glasses with whiskers

The Collar of Chaos

Mismatched fingerless gloves – this one is studded

Utility belt with cat-head pouch and cat tails on chain

Striped catsuit

Boots with cat-claw-shaped heels

Clawesome cuff
One of Cat Tastrophe's silver studded cuffs has a rat crawling up the side.

Cat of chaos
The cover of *Cat Tastrophe* Issue #1 shows the bad cat escaping through a window. It looks like she's falling, but she always lands on her feet.

"This job is so easy when the good guys are so gullible."

FREAKY FACT
Cat Tastrophe is an expert gymnast with supernatural balance and speed. She also wears the Collar of Chaos, which boosts her ability to spread disorder.

DRACULAURA
Licorice nightmare

Melting licorice bow

Black and pink drippy licorice earrings

Pigtails are wrapped in licorice

Black, elbow-length glove made of licorice

Fanged licorice-heart purse

Black-and-pink melting hem on skirt

Red fishnet socks

Shoes with sticky-looking melting heel

On a creepover at Frankie's, Draculaura's legendary sweet fang and her need for a midnight snack lead her to a dusty old box of sweets in Frankenstein's lab. Unfortunately, its main ingredient is the stuff of nightmares...

Bat's tasty!
Draculaura's pet bat, Count Fabulous, has been turned into a boiled sweet.

FREAKY FACT
Draculaura's sweet fang is famous at Monster High. All the ghouls and mansters know that Draculaura's locker is the go-to place for treats. It's a good thing vampires don't get cavities!

Eye heart you
Draculaura's eyes have been transformed into cute heart shapes, but there is nothing lovely about this nightmare scenario.

Ice-scream cone crown

ABBEY BOMINABLE
Ice scream, you scream...

Melting Skullette ice scream

Abbey finds that she has been drawn into a nightmare not of her own making and something is preventing her from waking up. Her clothes and accessories have been transformed to resemble an ice-scream sundae but, Abbey being Abbey, she refuses to panic.

"I must have plan to get out of this mess, but where first to start I haven't a guess."

Sundae handbag

Ice-scream underskirt with sprinkle pattern

Waffle cone skirt

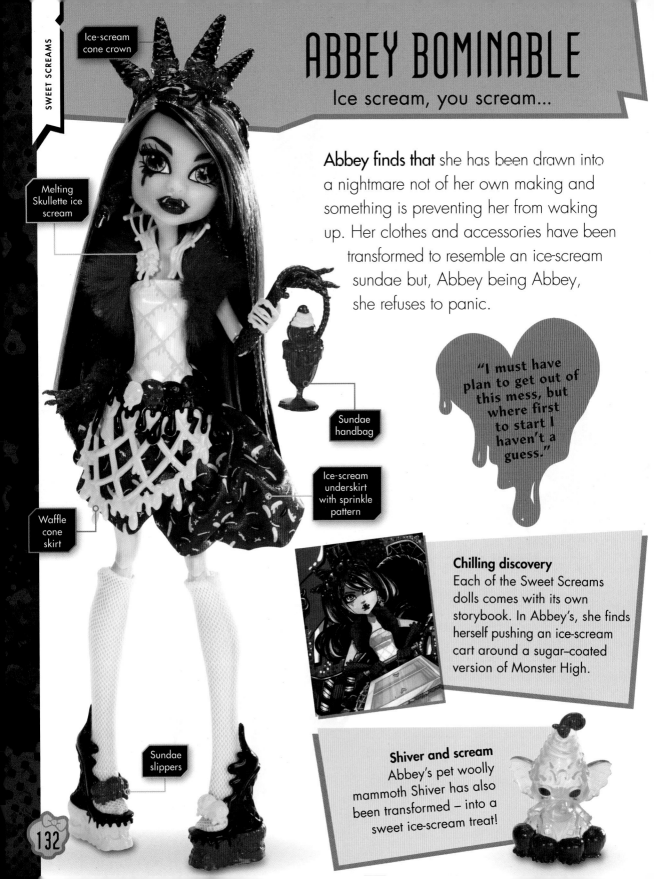

Chilling discovery
Each of the Sweet Screams dolls comes with its own storybook. In Abbey's, she finds herself pushing an ice-scream cart around a sugar–coated version of Monster High.

Sundae slippers

Shiver and scream
Abbey's pet woolly mammoth Shiver has also been transformed – into a sweet ice-scream treat!

FRANKIE STEIN
Candy calamity

Striped, boiled sweet hairpiece

Toffee-apple coat

Sticky sweet bag with a creepy iced face

Striped dress with tinsel hem

Melting red shoe straps

Frankie has had many creepovers at her house but none of them have ever turned into the kind of nightmare this one has. Draculaura's need for a midnight treat casts everyone into the same sticky situation, and the ghouls will have to work together to unwrap the mystery and wake up.

"How did I get here, this isn't right, I didn't eat candy at all last night!"

A sweet sole
Frankie's sweet shoes can't be the easiest to walk in – the soles are made of gloopy melting sugar!

Dog treat
Frankie's dog, Watzit, has turned into a canine confection with peppermint-cane legs. His ears look like the twists on a sweet wrapper.

GHOULIA YELPS
Ghastly gummy

Gummy worm and brains hairband

Dripping gummy frames

Sick-tummy gummy-bear bag

Neon-coloured worm print

Melting sweets belt

Shoes have gummy-worm straps

Ghoulia is locked in a classroom doing her beast to find a way out of a sugar-coated dream. She has no luck, and knows that unless she gets some help from her ghoulfriends, everyone at Monster High will be stuck in the dream forever.

Sweet accessories
Ghoulia is shocked when she finds she is wearing a pair of pink, gummy-worm earrings.

Trick or trapped?
Ghoulia tries everything she can think of to wake everyone up, but no matter what potion or scheme she concocts, nothing seems to work.

Sweet owl
Sir Hoots A Lot has been turned into a clear sweet with gummy ears and feet.

"I find this situation discomforting at best, like a subject I have not studied yet still must pass the test."*
*Translated from Zombie-speak

134

HONEY SWAMP
Marionette monster

Honey Swamp and some of the other ghouls are organising a circus-themed fundraiser to help save Monster High's arts programme. Budding filmmaker Honey is ready to step out from behind the camera with a marionette puppet act that is sure to slay the crowd... if she can learn the ropes in time!

Marionette strings attach to crosspiece

Scary-cool exaggerated circus make-up

Bootiful balloons
A translucent balloon necklace hangs around Honey's neck.

Pooch purse
Honey's circus look is complete with a handbag shaped like a balloon dog.

Stripy, circus big-top-inspired skirt overlay

All tied up in knots
Honey gets in a tangle rehearsing her routine, but luckily her friends' help comes with no strings attached.

Lace-up boots have pink balloons on the soles

JINAFIRE LONG
Fire-eating dragon

Flaming green fan to twirl

Headband with flame details

The Freak du Chic circus has arrived at Monster High – and Jinafire has joined! Fire-eating comes naturally to a dragon like Jinafire, but fire twirling is another matter entirely! Hopefully her patience will guide her through the flames.

Chequered circus-inspired dress with striped underskirt

Flaming footwear
Jinafire's shoes are dragon-inspired, with nostrils at the front and indents at the side, like eyes. The heels are flaming fans.

Twisting twirl
Some of the skills that make Jinafire a great designer will make her a fangtastic fire twirler, too. Both take patience, care and precision.

Pink sandals with tassels

TORALEI
The cat's meow

Theatrical fascinator

When Toralei volunteers for the Freak du Chic fundraiser, the other ghouls are surprised. But Toralei is willing to work with others to save the arts at Monster High. She'll need every ounce of her werecat grace to navigate the tightrope and ride a unicycle!

Spider-web umbrella with cat ears

Shredded circus dress

Cat walk
Toralei uses an umbrella for balance as she walks along the tightrope – just in case the old saying about werecats always landing on their feet isn't true.

"Eww! What's this positive, flowery feeling I'm having inside?!"

Wedges have cat heads on front and rope straps

Unicycle heel on shoes

137

FRANKIE STEIN
Monster magician

Frankie is always problem-solving, so it is this clever ghoul who suggests a fundraising dance and circus show to save the arts programme at Monster High. With help from circus-expert Gooliope, Frankie is ready to master some illusions if it means putting on a great show.

Magician's top hat

Skullette chain for a magic trick

Hypnotic dress to distract the eye

Magical boots
The heels on Frankie's boots are rabbits popping out of a top hat.

Striped overskirt

Knee-high boots

In the spotlight
Being stylishly stitched together comes in handy for magic tricks like this one.

FREAKY FACT
Frankie's Skullette chain trick involves the links magically pulling apart and coming back together with a touch of her wand.

138

TWYLA
Balancing boogey monster

Twyla realises that sometimes a ghoul has to step outside her comfort zone and into centre stage to save her school. Twyla stands tall on a pair of stilts in an act that balances on, well, balancing. Even with a shaky start, she's sure she can pull this off and help keep the arts at Monster High.

Sad clown make-up

Clown-inspired ruff

Fishnet sleeves

Jumpsuit with puffed shorts

Fishnet sock has drapes

Stilts are shadowy shapes

Circus chic
Stilt-walking Twyla comes with a poster showing off her monstrously magnificent circus style.

Twyla Boogeyman

FREAKY FACT
Twyla has made an effort to spend less time hiding and more time trying new things. Stilt-walking and a trip to circus school are definitely the most interesting things she's attempted.

Matching pet
Dustin the dust bunny is a pale aqua-green colour rather than the usual lavender.

139

Headpiece with miniature jester's hat

Balloons attached to spider-web string

ROCHELLE GOYLE
Mime magnifique

Clown-inspired ruffle

Rochelle may not know much about being a mime artist, but this gargoyle does know a thing or two about standing as still as a stone! She takes a crash course in circus performance and learns to mime to help save the arts at Monster High.

A monsterific mime
Rochelle takes a well-deserved bow after learning to mime her way out of an invisible box – in no time!

Dress with striped bodice and harlequin skirt

Bow-draped heels

Roll up! Roll up!
The circus has come to Monster High! This playset has a funhouse mirror, a strongman cutout for taking pictures, a tightrope and a swing.

CLAWDEEN WOLF
Lion-tamer extraordinaire

Miniature top hat

Faux-fur shrug looks like a lion's mane

Clawdeen knows that only the bravest acts and most daring stunts will get the ghouls the donations they need to save the arts programme. Her fierce and fearless lion taming just might be what they need to tip the scales in their favour.

FREAKY FACT

The arts programme at Monster High are very important to Clawdeen. She takes as many art classes as she can to make sure that her fashion designs are the best they can be.

Flaming hoop for lion to jump through

Zebra-print leggings

Theatrical sheer skirt strip

Over-the-knee lace-up boots

Crescent the "lion"
It's hard to get a lion on short notice, so Clawdeen did what she could with her pet cat and some faux fur.

DRACULAURA
Fashionista with monster ancestry

Skeletonised top hat

Lace parasol can open and close

There's no mistaking that Draculaura is monster royalty with her ultra-luxurious, spider-web-inspired look. This special collectors' doll is taller than usual, has killer poseability and comes with a special diary in a creepy-cool, coffin-shaped box.

Black-and-white bow tie

"I mean he [Dracula] was already a vampire back when togas were first considered fashionable... soooo glad Father doesn't wear one anymore."

Black spider-web-inspired cape

Pink spider-web stitching

Underskirt is shaped like a spider web

To-die-for eyelashes
This collectors' edition of Draculaura has rooted eyelashes and a special glazed-eye finish.

FRANKIE STEIN
New ghoul at the dance

Frankie's only been alive for a few weeks and already it's the Dawn of the Dance party! She spends the day putting together her most electrifying look – everything has to look perfect for her big debut!

Choker with bolt charm

Hot-pink shrug

Electric-blue cinch belt

Pink fishnet tights

Zigzag print on party dress matches hair

Mismatched shoes

Dawn of the Dance
It's the biggest party of the year! Frankie has a monsterific time at her first-ever party.

iCoffin
Like the other ghouls at Monster High, Frankie has a mobile phone to keep in touch with her friends.

FREAKY FACT
Frankie has a good heart but a lot to learn. Sometimes she makes mistakes (like pretending to have a boyfriend) because she wants to fit in with the older, more experienced ghouls.

CLAWDEEN WOLF
Clawesome fashionista

Two gold
earrings in
each ear

Being a fashionista isn't easy. When you have so many fur-ocious outfits, it's hard to choose the right one for the occasion. Luckily for Clawdeen, her best friend Draculaura is always willing to lend a hand (and an outfit) to help pull a party look together.

iCoffin is at
hand for
taking photos

Green
zip
clutch

Belt with
gold charms

Green belt
matches hair
and clutch

Hair-raising style
Being a werewolf makes Clawdeen's hair grow very fast. The electric-green bob with brown streaks she rocked at the dance will have grown out by Monday!

Zipped up
Clawdeen's hoodie dress has zip details, which are part of the aspiring fashion designer's signature style.

Green
fishnet tights

Gold metallic
heels match
zip detailing
on outfit

144

Glitter gel in hair

CLEO DE NILE
Queen of the night

Bronze choker with scarab charm

For Cleo, the self-proclaimed Queen of Monster High, there's nothing like a dance to remind her subjects why she's the most popular ghoul in school. With a shockingly stylish outfit and the most popular boy in school as her date, Cleo de Nile is ready to rule the night.

Exotic bronze cuff bracelet

Sleeve has wrap detail

Regal jewellery
Cleo's servants helped her pick out these Egyptian-inspired earrings. Cleo believes they enhance her regal bearing.

One-sleeve bandage dress

Bronze legging on one leg

FREAKY FACT
Cleo calls Deuce and Ghoulia several times on the day of the dance. She wants to make sure they are getting ready and will leave on time!

Pyramid handbag
Cleo's pyramid-shaped handbag is the perfect accessory for a true Egyptian princess. The bag even matches the pyramids dangling from her heels.

Emerald shoes with hanging pyramid details

DEUCE GORGON
Rockin' manster

Gold shades instead of his usual red pair

Hooded waistcoat

Scale-print shirt with tie

iCoffin clipped to belt

Black rose for Cleo

Pinstripe trousers with braces

White loafers for dancing

The school dance isn't enough to stress this chilled-out manster. After all, Deuce has the right clothes, the most clawesome ghoulfriend, Cleo and designer shades to keep his powers under control. He has everything he needs to make this night seriously clawesome.

Tamed snake-hawk
Deuce's green snakes are slicked back for a more formal look. Cleo will be impressed!

"Totally ready to rock!"

FREAKY FACT
The gold shades aren't just a fashion statement. Unless Deuce wants to turn everyone at Monster High to stone, he has to wear a pair with every outfit.

DRACULAURA
Party ghoul

Draculaura loves any excuse to have a party, but school dances are especially exciting. Her favourite part is fanging out with her friends, trading clothes, getting ready and taking lots of selfies – of course!

"Clawdeen came over and we had an expedition through my closet to find outfits for both of us. We only had to go back two centuries to find what we needed."

Mini heart-shaped hat with fascinator

Dangling heart earrings

Strapless striped dress with ruffle trim

Sparkly pink bow-shaped clutch

Ends of satin bow hang down

Bootiful bow
Hot-pink satin shoulder covers tie in a bow at the back of Draculaura's dress.

Draculaura hearts heels
Draculaura's shoes have fangtastic heart-shaped pink heels. She is ready to party!

Black-and-pink heels

147

GHOULIA YELPS
Ready to party... finally!

Creating the perfect dance look is a marathon, not a sprint – and no one knows that better than Ghoulia. It may take her all day to find the right look, style it to perfection and make it out the door, but she always looks drop-dead gorgeous.

Skull on sash matches skull earrings

iCoffin – Ghoulia is always prepared!

Bone-print clutch

White-to-pink sparkly dress

"I have assembled three outfits, each have their own strengths and weaknesses. It only takes me two hours to decide."*

*Translated from Zombie-speak

FREAKY FACT

Being a slow-moving daughter of zombies means that sudden changes are sometimes really hard for Ghoulia. She always leaves herself plenty of time to make big decisions.

Glittery white fishnet tights

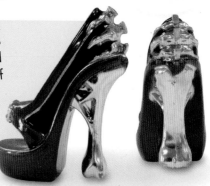

Party peeptoes
Ghoulia's shiny red shoes have a set of shockingly cool silver bones for the heels.

LAGOONA BLUE
Scary-cute sea chic

Lagoona is all set to make a splash at Dawn of the Dance with her fin-tastic dress and all her best ghoulfriends at her side. She spends the morning soaking in her hydration station, so she'll look and feel her best when she is dancing on dry land.

Mohawk looks like a fish fin

Pearl necklace

Golden wrap bracelet

Aqua-some accessory
This shimmery, clam-shaped handbag has a pretty pearl handle. The shell shape mirrors the clam detail on Lagoona's sash.

Fishnet sash

Mermaid-style dress

"Be natural. Be yourself and you'll be spot-on."

FREAKY FACT
Lagoona takes her hair inspiration from the sea for Dawn of the Dance. This is the only Lagoona doll to feature a Mohawk.

Sheer heels with ombre effect

149

DRACULAURA
Fun in the sun(screen)

The only thing that could make Draculaura more excited for Fearleading Mashionals is a trip to the beach! With her Fear Squad beasties at her side, she's ready to cheer her heart out and spend a few days lounging on Gloom Beach. All she needs is SPF 500 sunscreen and an umbrella to keep her skin safe from the sun.

Pink sunglasses match her highlights

Heart-print swimsuit

Sunscreen is always close at hand

Polka-dot wrap with bow fastening

Sandals with pink and yellow bows

Fearless fearleader
With her boundless energy and enthusiasm, this vampire puts her all into fearleading.

Simply bow-tiful
Draculaura loves adding cute little bow features on her outfits. Her earrings are tiny bows too!

FREAKY FACT
As a porcelain-skinned vampire, Draculaura always has to carry sunscreen to prevent her from getting serious sunburn.

CLAWDEEN WOLF
Beast on the beach

Fangtastic yellow sunglasses

There's no place to fang out during spring break that's quite like Gloom Beach. It has everything a ghoul and manster could want: sand, water, screech volleyball and absolutely no homework in sight.

Rainbow leopard monokini

Wish you were here!
Each Gloom Beach doll comes with a postcard, showing them having a clawesome time in beach gear that suits their individual styles.

Frisbee – for beach fun with her beasties

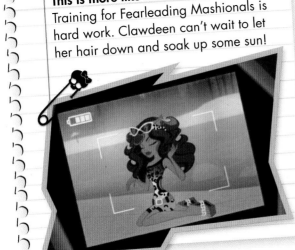

This is more like it...
Training for Fearleading Mashionals is hard work. Clawdeen can't wait to let her hair down and soak up some sun!

Pink-and-gold sandals have chain straps

151

FRANKIE STEIN
Beach lightning

Frankie worked so hard to get on the school fearleading squad. With all that practice under her belt, she's ready to compete at Gloom Beach, then spend the rest of her break relaxing and enjoying the beach with her ghoulfriends.

Lightning-bolt, one-piece swimsuit

Beach bag has a lightning-bolt bottom

Tartan cover-up

Yellow sandals with blue buckles

Jump-start the party!
Just like her outfit, Frankie's beach bag is electric, with handles made from striking red and blue jump leads.

Sun, sand... but no surf
Although Frankie won't take a dip in the sea for fear of giving the other swimmers an electric shock, she loves to enjoy a day on the shore.

Electric blue
Frankie's shades have jagged, lightning-bolt frames. Their cool blue colour matches her other beach accessories.

CLEO DE NILE
Fearleading captain

Being the captain of the Fear Squad can be a lot of pressure for Cleo. She wants her team to win and she works them hard to make it happen. So when the time comes to enjoy the beach, this princess is first in line for some relaxation.

Oversized teal sunglasses

Gold, wrap-style swimsuit

Fan in the shape of a papyrus plant

Teal wrap matches sunglasses and sandals

Ancient earrings
Cleo tries to show off her scaritage whenever she can, so her earrings are shaped like the Egyptian pyramids.

Striped legwarmer looks like mummy wrappings

Leader of ghouls
Although the other ghouls are calm, Cleo can't help worrying. She knows they have the biggest cheer of their unlives ahead of them, and she wants to be ready.

Teal, brick-effect wedges

153

Orange shutter shades

JACKSON JEKYLL
Just a normal day at the beach...

Sleeveless collared shirt

Jackson loves school but he's been looking forward to spring break at Gloom Beach for weeks. All he wants is some fun, maybe a tan and the chance to spend more time with Frankie Stein, the new ghoul in school. Who knows, maybe sparks will fly between them...

Board shorts have a black half and a chequered half

Black-and-white volleyball

"Just because I'm not a monster, doesn't mean I can't party like one!"

Light and shade
Jackson's volleyball is a yin-yang symbol, referencing his split personality.

Beach bros
Jackson's friend Deuce is at a Gorgon family reunion on the island of Petros, in Greece. Jackson writes him a postcard, saying that Gloom Beach is creeperific and he's missing out.

Flip-flops with Skullette detail

154

GHOULIA YELPS
Sleeps like the undead

Red bow on pyjama top

Black skirt with striped waistband

Blood-splatter-print pyjamas

Glasses on slippers match Ghoulia's own

After a busy week of studies at Monster High, the girls are dead tired and in need of some relaxation. Ghoulia and the rest of the ghouls gather for a night of games, makeovers and ghoul time at the home of Ghoulia's BFF, Cleo.

Online umpire
Ghoulia likes to bring her laptop to creepovers. She acts as referee when the other ghouls can't agree on the rules of the game.

Fright bites
Ghoulia brings brain puffs, a popular monster snack, for all the ghouls to share.

155

CLEO DE NILE
Dream of the Nile

Cleo is known for hosting amazing creepovers. She loves organising makeovers, fanging out and playing her favourite board game "Gargoyles to Gargoyles". The other ghouls quickly learn that competitive Cleo takes winning the game very seriously.

Eyemask with Egyptian Eye of Horus symbol

Arm wrappings

Casual, bandage-print pyjamas

Crowns decorate slippers

A worthy opponent
The ghouls often let Cleo win at games. But Cleo is thrilled to have finally faced a true challenge when Abbey beats her.

Rays of light
Cleo carries a pyramid-shaped nightlight to ease her fear of the dark.

FRANKIE STEIN

A monster in the morning

Being invited to her first creepover is so exciting for Frankie. She's ready to stay up all night sharing secrets and doing her nails. And with all her beasties there to keep her charged up, she knows it will be the best slumber party ever.

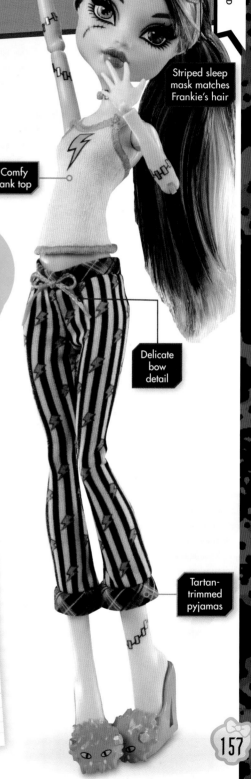

Striped sleep mask matches Frankie's hair

Comfy tank top

Delicate bow detail

Tartan-trimmed pyjamas

Party tunes
Frankie brings her iCoffin docking station and speakers with her, so the ghouls can dance the night away.

"Sometimes we just need to stay up all night and catch up."

Electric alarm
Frankie begins each day with a start, because she normally sleeps in a power generator. It's a real energy boost!

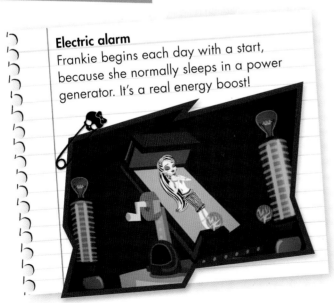

DRACULAURA
Rest in peace

Hair tied back, ready for bed

Ruffled sleep top

Tub of ice scream

Draculaura has been to a lot of slumber parties in her 1600 years, but having fun never gets old. Draculaura's favourite creepover game is Truth or Scare. It helps her to learn all the juicy secrets everyone is keeping, and they usually do a few silly scares.

Eternal sleep
Draculaura always gets a good night's sleep inside her coffin-bed playset. Coffins are comfortable and cosy, and they come in different styles to suit every vampire's needs.

"I'm bringing scary human boovies!"

Bed head
An earlier Dead Tired Draculaura doll comes with polka-dot pyjamas and pigtails. She was released in the first wave of Dead Tired dolls.

Pink monster slippers with bat ears

158

LAGOONA BLUE
Laid-back monster

Eye mask on elastic strap

Lagoona loves any chance to kick back and enjoy a night with her ghoulfriends. As much fun as she has with the swim team and her boyfriend, Gil, Lagoona always makes time to bond with her beasties.

This Skullette also wears a sleep mask

Lagoona's mug of hot cocoa is flavoured with seaweed – her favourite!

"Creepovers are the beast way to find out your ghoulfriends aren't shallow."

Pyjama shorts printed with scales

Hydration station
Lagoona takes daily dips in this hydration station playset, to keep her sensitive skin from drying out on land. It leaves her feeling refreshed for the night ahead.

Turquoise slippers with pink fins

FRANKIE STEIN

She's got this all sewn up

Scissor earrings

Top made from mismatched material

Homemade Watzit toy

Pincushion bracelet

Ruffle trim on apron

Tights in Frankie's signature tartan

Exposed red seam

Frankie's mismatched body parts are the perfect inspiration for her Home Ick class projects. Her strict teacher, Ms Kindergrübber, expects a lot from her students, so Frankie helps her classmates by creating a Home Ick survival guide.

"Okay – if you follow my advice you'll never fall apart in this class."

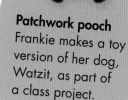

Patchwork pooch
Frankie makes a toy version of her dog, Watzit, as part of a class project.

Model student
Frankie's sewing skills mean she can create new looks. She stores an outfit change in her locker playset, and turns the classroom into a catwalk.

LAGOONA BLUE
A+ assistant

Lagoona has to pass Mad Science before she gets to study her favourite subject, Ocean-ogre-phy. The teacher, Mr Hackington, has a scary reputation, but Lagoona knows if she follows his lab rules, the class will be smooth sailing.

Plaited hair stays clear of chemicals

Anchor earrings

Lab coat, in case of spills

Beaker with frog

Anchor and bubble print

Study notes
Lagoona's doll comes with two versions of her class notes – one small enough for her locker and one human-sized.

Experimental egg
This egg looks like a harmless fossil, but beware! It could be an unhatched gargoyle.

Teacher's pets
Lagoona feels a close connection with the laboratory frogs. Like her, frogs can live on land or in the water.

Shoes have long ankle straps

161

GHOULIA YELPS
She's got deadly aim

Monster
High school
logo

Coordinating
sweatband

Dodgeball
with
Skullette

Loose black
shorts are worn
over a longer,
stretchy pair

Platform
trainers

Zombies are dead famous for being slow movers, so dodgeball seems an odd sport for Ghoulia. Her Physical Deaducation class teaches her that skill is what counts on the playing field. With her perfect aim, foolproof strategy and laser focus she is not to be underestimated.

*"Poor skills coupled with a good attitude will earn you a better grade than the reverse."**
*Translated from Zombie-speak

Sporty style
Ghoulia's cat's-eye glasses are held on by a red headband so they stay in place when she is playing.

Ghouls in the gym
After her Physical Deaducation class, Ghoulia hits the locker room, grabs a drink of water and changes into a dress.

162

CLEO DE NILE
Betrayed princess

The once-in-1,300 years blooming of the Corpse Flower brings back painful memories for Cleo. The last time she saw it she was trapped in her tomb, abandoned by a friend. This time, she's dressed up and determined to see the flower bloom at the Gloom and Bloom dance, surrounded by her true ghoulfriends.

Egyptian lotus flower headband

Egyptian gold choker

Patterned bag holds golden garden tools

Egyptian-style striped sash

Gold heels with lotus flower decoration

Amanita Nightshade
Amanita pretended to be Cleo's friend 1,300 years ago, but left her stranded. Cleo is not happy to see her again – when she blooms from the Corpse Flower!

Ferocious flower
This lotus plant is not what it seems! Lift it up and its roots are a creepy-cool cobra coiled underneath.

163

Fancy flytrap hairpiece

VENUS MCFLYTRAP
She really grows on you

Venus loves all of Mother Earth's plants, but there's something special about the Corpse Flower. With everyone gathering in their most plantastic outfits to celebrate the flower's bloom, Venus is excited to watch monster history happen.

Black vine earrings

Twisting vine decoration

Green vine cuff

Surprise guest
Venus McFlytrap welcomes Amanita Nightshade as she blooms from the Corpse Flower. Amanita is happy to see the monsters throwing her a party!

Flytrap-print dress

Flytrap leg wrap

Fangtastic flytrap
This flora-loving plant monster is never far from a plant. Venus has a potted venus flytrap and a creepy vine-covered watering can for looking after it.

Boots have spiked heels

GLOOM AND BLOOM

JANE BOOLITTLE
Blossoming beauty

Striking floral headpiece

Feather earrings

Tropical floral-print top

Belt with Skullette and feather details

Black feather skirt

Tropical hibiscus flowers wrap around ankles

Strappy sandals with pebble heels

Dances and social gatherings make Jane anxious, but something as monumental as the Corpse Flower's arrival at Monster High can't be missed. Besides, Jane couldn't let the gore-geous dress Jinafire made for her go unworn!

Monster mash
Jinafire designed Jane's Gloom and Bloom outfit to mash the garden theme with Jane's jungle-island background.

Party plant
Jane's plant for the Gloom and Bloom dance has Skullette roots. Her trowel matches the flowers and Jane's other accessories.

165

CATRINE DEMEW
Purrfectly-styled partygoer

Deep-blue flower headband

Catrine has seen her share of parties at Monster High, but the Gloom and Bloom dance is bigger than anything that has come before! With a dress designed by her dear friend Jinafire, artsy Catrine is ready to paint the school red in anticipation of the Corpse Flower blooming.

Green choker with bow

Black corsage

Lily-print, double-layered dress

Werecat worries
Even sophisticated city ghouls like Catrine feel insecure sometimes. Getting ready for the dance leaves her worrying about how others see her freaky flaws.

Flowering-vine cuffs

Freaky flowerpot
Catrine's potted plant has spiky leaves and pink flowers with monster faces, and the roots are wrapped around a heart. Her trowel is shaped like a claw.

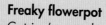

Blue stilettos with flower straps

JINAFIRE LONG
Designer dragon

Topknot decorated with red flower comb

Lotus flower shoulder details

Fan-shaped bag

Colourful silk dress with gold flower pattern

Overskirt has Chinese dragon print

Shoes have detachable cuffs with a fan and flower design

Jinafire loves to design clothing, and the rare blooming of the Corpse Flower has given her the idea to create floral fashions that seem to blossom with a life of their own. For each ghoul's look, she combines the floral theme with the ghouls' unique styles.

"I have been asked by Jane, Venus, Catrine and Cleo to design their dresses for the Gloom and Bloom dance."

Scarily stylish

Jinafire's plant comes in a bootiful vase with dragons for handles, which hints at what lies beneath. The plant's roots are a black dragon's head!

PYXIS PREPSTOCKINGS
Polo-playing pegasus

Blue riding hat with chinstrap

Preppy pink polo shirt

Horseshoe print on left hind leg

First-place ribbon skirt

Rosettes decorate leg protectors

Pyxis is a hybrid creature called a Fright-Mare, who was formed when a pegasus merged with a nightmare in the faraway Dream Pastures. Perfectly polished Pyxis moves the same way as she speaks – precisely, with not a word or hoof out of place.

FREAKY FACT
Fright-Mares were once ordinary nightmares. In the Dream Pastures, they became monster hybrids and now carry dreams to the monster species they are linked with.

MONSTER HYBRID:
Pegasus

DREAM PASTURE HOME:
A well-manicured hill in the centre of the pasture.

DREAM JOB:
Organising perfect pegasus dreams

BFFs: Aery Evenfall, Skyra Bouncegait

FRETS QUARTZMANE
Galloping gargoyle

Bat-like gargoyle wings

When **Frets Quartzmane** landed in the Dream Pastures, music announced her arrival. This rocking Fright-Mare shapes dreams with tunes from her pan flute, and her gargoyle side makes her a solid friend.

Gothic black rose

MONSTER HYBRID:
Gargoyle

DREAM PASTURE HOME:
Anywhere she can blare out loud rock music.

DREAM JOB:
Using her musical abilities to create sweet dreams.

BFFs: Penepole Steamtail, Bay Tidechaser

Speckled skin looks like granite stone

"It's all about the hoof beats for me. I'm always trotting out the latest tunes."

Green fin matches flowing hair

BAY TIDECHASER
Monster from the deep

Fresh from being caught up in the wash of a sea monster's dream, Bay crashed into the Dream Pastures like a monster wave. She is as untamed as the ocean itself, but is never stormy with her friends. Bay dwells where the Dream Pastures meets the water.

Seahorse emblem on pink top

"I unlive for the ocean wind in my mane and the waves on my hoofs."

Coral and seashells decorate skirt

Sea-monster fin at end of tail

MONSTER HYBRID:
Sea monster

DREAM PASTURE HOME:
On the shore – ready to surf when the waves come in.

DREAM JOB:
Calming the storms of sea-monster dreams.

BFFs: Aery Evenfall, Fawntine Fallowhart

Golden leg protectors decorated with rope and coral

170

AERY EVENFALL
Skeletal Fright-Mare

Two-tone hair is pink and black

Aery has stars in her eyes

Skeletal wings

Bone skirt

Constellation on left hind leg

Flaming, lace-up leg protectors

Skeleton-hybrid Aery watches the night skies for Fright-Mares falling into her world like fiery bolts of lightning. It is her job to welcome the newly created Fright-Mares and help them adjust to unlife in the Dream Pastures.

FREAKY FACT

The only monsters, besides the Fright-Mares, who can reach the Dream Pastures are Twyla and her father, the Boogeyman.

MONSTER HYBRID:
Skeleton

DREAM PASTURE HOME:
Aery is a wanderer, always watching the night sky for new arrivals.

DREAM JOB:
Making sure skeletons find their way back to their dream closets.

BFFs: Aery is a friend to all Fright-Mares.

PENEPOLE STEAMTAIL
Beastly butterfly

Removable screampunk goggles

Cogs and wheels decorate metallic wings

Customised skirt, with chains, cogs and a horseshoe

Laced-up leg protectors

Penepole is a butterfly hybrid with a love of all things robotic and screampunk. A clockwork enthusiast, she believes precision makes the world go round, and that includes getting her name right. It's P-E-N-E-P-O-L-E!

MONSTER HYBRID:
Butterfly

DREAM PASTURE HOME:
A clock tower

DREAM JOB:
Making dreams run like clockwork.

BFFs:
Frets Quartzmane, Pyxis Prepstockings

"I'm a finely tuned Fright-Mare who's geared to trot like a top."

SKYRA BOUNCEGAIT
Ghostly fearleader

Skyra was created in the dream of a ghost – a ghost who just happened to be on her school's fearleading team. This makes Skyra relentlessly upbeat and full of spirit, always urging on the rest of the herd to: "Go! Fright! Win!"

"I've been accused of being 'perky' but I prefer to think of myself as energetic."

Hair in high ponytails

Fearleading vest with upside-down horseshoe

Accessories are all in team colours

Leg protectors feature pom-pom balls

Fearleader megaphone mark on left hind leg

MONSTER HYBRID:
Ghost

DREAM PASTURE HOME:
Skyra's spirit is everywhere.

DREAM JOB:
Raising the spirits of ghost dreamers.

BFFs:
Penepole Steamtail, Aery Evenfall

173

FAWNTINE FALLOWHEART
Rare woodland beast

Dear Fawntine is a deer-spirit hybrid. She nurtures everything, alive or undead, in the forest. She's kind, quiet, a little mysterious and rarely leaves her forest home unless a full gathering of Fright-Mares is called.

"My friends say I'm a little bit quiet and a little bit shy and they're a little bit right."

Skeleton birds perch on Fawntine's antlers

Antler-styled eyebrows

Mossy green streaks in hair

Tufty deer tail

Ivy-green vines encircle waist

Twisting-vine leg protectors

MONSTER HYBRID:
Deer spirit

DREAM PASTURE HOME:
The deep forests of the Dream Pastures.

DREAM JOB:
Bringing calm to anxious deer spirits' dreams.

BFFs: Aery Evenfall, Bay Tidechaser

FLARA BLAZE
Phoenix-like fire elemental

Flaming purple Mohawk

As a fire elemental hybrid, Flara is as unpredictable as the element she represents. Flara can change a dream from warm and comforting one moment to a raging inferno the next, depending on which way the wind, or her mood, blows.

Burnished brass wings

Fabulous feathered collar

MONSTER HYBRID:
Fire elemental

DREAM PASTURE HOME:
An area of hot springs, geysers and lava.

DREAM JOB:
Creating a spark and transforming dreams.

BFFs: Free-spirit Flara is her own best friend.

Burning-feather leg protectors

Mini orange flames form her tail

FREAKY FACT
Elementals are monsters linked to one of the elements, such as fire. Holt Hyde and Heath Burns are fire elementals.

175

TWO GHOUL FOR SCHOOL

Whether it is fanging out with their BFF or going to the dance with their favourite manster, the ghouls of Monster High know that unlife is more fun with friends. These scary pairs are all perfectly matched.

Frankie and Jackson both have yellow-streaked hair

Jackson's yellow glasses match Frankie's yellow accessories

Neon-yellow lightning bolt earrings

Casual, grey-checked cardigan

Yin-yang symbol on Jackson's shirt

Creepy-cute yellow bow

Silver picnic-casket handbag

Electric-blue, stitched tartan skirt

FREAKY FACT

One of Frankie and Jackson's ill-fated dates was ruined when Jackson's alter ego, Holt Hyde, turned up and spoilt the mood.

Grey, slip-on loafers

FRANKIE STEIN AND JACKSON JEKYLL

Is love in the air?

Jackson is always trying to plan a quiet outing with Frankie, but his plans keep getting wrecked. Meanwhile, Frankie really wants to like Jackson. He's scary sweet, creepy cute and the nicest normie she knows – apart from the fact that he has a habit of standing her up. Frankie is an understanding ghoul, but she has her limits!

Meet cute
Frankie and Jackson's past dates have included busy boovie theatres and malls. Their picnic is by far a more successful, and quieter, affair.

Matching stripes
Frankie and Jackson are already fashionably in sync – they both wear matching double stripes on their sleeves.

Well-heeled
Sparks fly on Frankie and Jackson's date, thanks to Frankie's electric-themed shoes. Frankie's black heels have bright-pink bolt heels.

"Me? Why would I make you nervous? I'm the one that gets nervous."
– Frankie, to Jackson

Venus

Rochelle

Hair fastened back with a green vine hair bobble

Candy-floss striped hair

Earring has intricate berry and leaf details

Cracked skin due to virus

Twisting vine bracelets wrap around Venus's finger

Lily clasp at centre of belt

Stained-glass design on handbag

Both girls wear similar tulle dresses

Shoes have thorny heels and a fanged-smirk decoration on toes

180

VENUS MCFLYTRAP AND ROCHELLE GOYLE

Zombie-infected monsters

When a zombie-themed dance is planned at Monster High, no one imagines that it will involve anything more than a fashion change – until Ghoulia accidentally releases a virus that turns the student disembody into the dancing undead. Now Venus and Rochelle have been infected, and they can't stop dancing to drop-dead beats!

Going viral
Ghoulia's virus is transmitted by contact. A simple high five is enough to transform Rochelle, and soon the dancing is out of control.

Hair-brained
Venus's half-shaved zombie-themed hairstyle reveals a creepy-cool brain design!

FREAKY FACT

As well as causing uncontrollable dancing, the zombie virus even makes Rochelle and Venus's handwriting styles resemble Ghoulia's!

Dancing shoes
Rochelle is ready to dance all night in these gothic, gargoyle-design heeled boots. She just didn't know when she put them on that she might have to dance forever!

Ghoulia

Cleo

Headband fastens hair back from face

Cobra safety goggles

White lab coat with red brain pattern on cuffs and collar

Beaker bubbling with red perfume

Hidden sparkles on edge of lab coat resemble DNA

Bright periodic-table print

Animal print on edge of lab coat

FREAKY FACT

Even though Cleo sometimes treats Ghoulia as if she's her assistant, the pair really do have a genuine, deep friendship.

Lace-up wedges with brain-pattern heels

Open-toe platform wedges

GHOULIA YELPS AND CLEO DE NILE

Study buddies

Ghoulia is the smartest ghoul in school. When partnered with Cleo on science projects, Ghoulia usually does all the work while Cleo somehow gets all the glory. This time, though, the topic is the science of perfume, and Cleo is, for once, really eager to get to work.

Perfume assignment fail
Not all of Cleo and Ghoulia's perfume experiments are wearable – for example, the batch that smells of troll cabbage and broccoli with none-too-subtle undertones of burned popcorn.

Friendship fashion
Cleo's earrings are three tiles with GH, F and F printed on them – for "Ghoul Friends Forever".

Making science
Ghoulia and Cleo have all of the vials, tubes and beakers they need to put the mad into science.

Elementally clawesome
Ghoulia's dress is decorated with the periodic table of elements, spelling out words such as "monster", "fab", "totally", "voltage", "scary", and "cute".

"One thing I am learning about Heath Burns is that when Heath says, 'I got this' it is meaning he does not."
– Abbey

Pink-striped hair worn in a high ponytail

Boney-finger tongs

Flames on sleeves of jacket are a design choice, not actual fire!

Flame design on T-shirt matches jacket and shoes

School apron with black bow and tulle edging

School apron embroidered with Monster High logo

FREAKY FACT
Heath was distracted when registering for classes, so instead of checking the box for Metal Shop he checked the one for Home Ick!

Heeled cowboy boots

Flame design on shoes completes a hot outfit

184

ABBEY BOMINABLE AND HEATH BURNS

Recipe for disaster

When Abbey encouraged Heath to take Home Ick, she didn't think it would mean having to team up with him for a class assignment. Now, her grade will depend on Heath not creating a huge mess and destroying their project.

Quality time
Even though Heath is not excited about cooking and sewing, he does look forward to spending time with Abbey in class.

Mixing it up
Abbey is well equipped for her Home Ick classes with her spatula and spoon earrings!

Fire starter
Even with his fiery powers contained by an oven mitt, Heath can't help but cause fires all over the place.

Tools of the trade
A measuring jug, a bone-handled spoon and an eyeball-topped cookie jar are all useful tools to have in the Home Ick classroom.

185

Shaved head hairstyle

Beehive hairstyle

Red brain hair corsage matches Slo Mo's flowers

Blood dripping from red bow tie

Skeletal-arm earrings

Skeleton ribcage printed on front of dinner jacket

Skull necklace

Bunch of flowers resembles brains

Purple stripe on edge of tuxedo trousers

Heart ribcage and arm pattern on prom dress

Blood-red strappy heels look like they're dripping

SLOMAN "SLO MO" MORTAVITCH AND GHOULIA YELPS

Prom-going pair

Ghoulia wants Slo Mo to ask her to the prom. She has been dropping hints like a rookie juggler on a unicycle but Slo Mo remains oblivious. Slo Mo may be a genius at maths, a champion at chess and co-captain of the Monster High casketball team, but he is completely unaware when it comes to matters of the heart.

Dead cute couple
Ghoulia and Slo Mo go together like vampires and coffins. It's said that true love never dies, and in the case of Slo Mo and Ghoulia, what's said is true.

Red eye
Behind her glasses, Ghoulia's irises have a red highlight that matches her cherry-red lipstick, outfit and accessories.

"I thought it was just another dance. Ghouls, however, do not think it is just another dance."
– Slo Mo
*Translated from Zombie-speak

Sharp dresser
Slo Mo's purple wingtip shoes have a spider-web detail on the heel that's spooky enough to match his skeleton jacket.

LAGOONA BLUE AND GILLINGTON "GIL" WEBBER
Skate date

Gil has been planning a big surprise for the anniversary of his first date with Lagoona. However, his track record of planning surprise dates for Lagoona is soggy at beast, as circumstances always seem to have a way of ruining his designs. Taking matters into her own hands, Lagoona plans a date to skate that sounds romantically simple and simply romantic.

Gold fin helmet secured by pearl strap beneath chin

Hair fastened back, away from face

Sparkly playsuit in a bubble pattern

Matching gold knee and elbow pads

Finned teal-and-gold skates

"I know that Gil wants to do all the planning, but I think it's about time for this ghoul to take the whale by the tail and do some planning herself." – Lagoona

FREAKY FACT
Gil and Lagoona will never forget their first date at the Monster High fountain. They still celebrate it every year.

Crash helmet comes with a hole for Gil's fin

Gil's gills are visible on his neck

Skullette elbow pads

Skullette knee pads

Roller skates mean Gil is ready to roll

Fish out of water

For ease when skating, Gil has traded his usual breathing helmet for a more streamlined, fin-shaped nose mask with goggles.

"Oh, manster. I had dinner cruise plans for our anniversary date all set; only I found out tonight that the boat sank at the docks."
– Gil

Scale-pattern trousers allow flexible movement

The perfect catch

Lagoona and Gil's romance was as inevitable as the tides. From the first time she saw him in class, Lagoona couldn't imagine herself with any other manster.

SDCC EXCLUSIVES

Every ghoul is unique, but some creepy characters are truly spooktacular! Since 2010, Monster High fans at San Diego Comic Con have been able to get their claws on these exclusive dolls.

FRANKIE STEIN
Movie star

This version of Frankie was the first Monster High doll to be featured as an exclusive at San Diego Comic Con (SDCC). The choice to present Frankie in greyscale in 2010 was an homage to the classic monster movies of the 1930s and 1940s – the same horror films that made her dad, Frankenstein, famous.

FREAKY FACT

Frankie's unusual blue and green eyes are black and white on this monotone version of her.

Skullette-head earrings

Polka-dot tie with Skullette tie tack

Black mesh underskirt

Studded bag with Skullette

Weird Watzit
Even Frankie's sparky canine companion, Watzit, has been given a monochrome makeover to match Frankie's.

Black-and-white spiked heels

GHOULIA YELPS
Cosplay comic fan

Glasses with nose resemble Dead Fast's mask

NekroCon pass on lanyard

Dead Fast figure, still in its box

DEADFAST

With her starring role at SDCC in 2011, comic fan Ghoulia took the opportunity to do a little cosplay. Dressed up as a character of her own invention, Ms Dead Fast, Ghoulia is all set for NekroCon – the biggest comic convention in the monster world.

Dead Fast belt decorated with brains

Sparkly black catsuit

DEADFAST

Comic artist
In her bag, Ghoulia carries a comic that she drew featuring the character Dead Fast and herself as his partner. She hopes it will impress the makers of Dead Fast at NekroCon!

BOOM!!!

Dead Fast tote bag holds NekroCon loot

Brain attack
Suitable for a zombie comic convention, Ghoulia's outfit is accessorised with brains. She wears red brain earrings to match her belt.

High-heeled version of Dead Fast's red boots

Olive green headband

Eyes have no visible pupils

SCARAH SCREAMS

Fan favourite

In 2011, fans voted for Scarah Screams to be the SDCC 2012 exclusive. As a banshee, Scarah has trouble communicating with the other students, as they're terrified that she is foretelling their deaths just by speaking to them. To get around this, she has studied ways of talking without speaking.

Olive green plastic belt

Shiny pleather miniskirt

FREAKY FACT

Scarah can read minds, having studied TSL (Telepathy as a Second Language) since she was a wee ghoul.

AGE:
15

DAUGHTER OF:
The bean si (Banshee)

KILLER STYLE:
Vintage pieces in olive green.

FREAKY FLAW: Scarah has a way of saying things that makes monsters believe something bad will happen.

BFFs: Hoodude Voodoo and Invisi Billy

Green platform heels

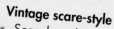

Vintage scare-style
Scarah rocks a creeperific vintage look, with her curled-under fringe and big barrel curls. Her hair is parted from the back into two distinct curls.

HOODUDE VOODOO
Scarah's plus-one

Letterman jacket

Different-coloured eyes, like Frankie's

Heart worn on chest

When fans voted for Scarah to be the SDCC 2012 exclusive, Scarah brought her beast friend, Hoodude, along too. Hoodude was created by Frankie to make the other ghouls think she had a boyfriend, but he embarked on his own unlife when she broke off their relationship.

AGE:
Let's just say he's 15

SON OF: Frankie (sort of)

KILLER STYLE:
Hoodude calls his style "floppy casual".

FREAKY FLAW:
Hoodude can be overly sensitive.

BFF: Scarah Screams

FREAKY FACT
Hoodude, like Scarah, was a character created for the Monster High webisodes who has since made the leap from digital to doll form.

Legs stitched together from rags

Ragtag ragdoll
Being a voodoo doll, when Hoodude has a bad day, everyone else does, too. Thankfully, he has had fewer bad days since his friend Scarah tied up some loose ends inside his brain.

WEBARELLA
Ambidextrous alter ego

Red spider-web earrings

Fingerless glove

Web-print halter-neck top

This super-hero spider was the SDCC 2013 exclusive – unusually before her regular monster alter ego, Wydowna, had even been released. She is on the Power Ghouls team, alongside Wonder Wolf, Voltageous, Polterghoul and Cat Tastrophe.

Spiky red bangle

Super-hero toolkit
Webarella's belt is decorated with a Webarella Skullette with six red eyes to match her own. Her silver lasso, which she uses to round up creepy crooks, hangs from a hook on her belt.

Red circle skirt

FREAKY FACT

Webarella's pet fly, Shoo, accompanies her on her crime-fighting missions. Shoo has huge silver eyes and wears a red chrome bow.

Sparkly silver, spider-web boots

Shoo

WYDOWNA SPIDER
Webarella's true form

Hairline styled in a widow's peak

Wydowna Spider began haunting the halls of Monster High in doll form right after the SDCC debut of her alter ego, Webarella. Wydowna chases grades instead of bad guys. Her interest in pop culture is reflected in her fashion choices.

Comic-book-print dress

Spurred along
The heels of Wydowna's silver boots have red spider-web-shaped spurs that spin just like the spurs on cowboy boots.

White messenger bag

Silver boots with spider-web pattern

AGE: 16

DAUGHTER OF: Arachne

KILLER STYLE: Wydowna likes to refer to her style as rock-and-roll geek.

FREAKY FLAW: She's such a multitasker, it's easy for her to get worn out.

BFFs: Ghoulia Yelps, Clawdeen Wolf

PET: Shoo

Spider style
Wydowna is a true fashionista, and loves making her own clothes out of the spider silk she spins. Her latest creation is a tunic dress with a punchy comic-book-style "splat" print.

One of two horns

MANNY TAUR
Bull on best behaviour

Red T-shirt with maze print

Manny has an established role as a bully, but for his debut doll appearance it was decided to give him more heart than horns. Therefore, at SDCC 2014, fans were treated to a softer side of Manny, plus a pairing with his ghoulfriend, Iris.

AGE:
16

SON OF: The Minotaur

KILLER STYLE:
Manny is a boo-collar manster who prefers jeans, T-shirts and work boots.

FREAKY FLAW:
Manny often breaks stuff, though not on purpose. He's a bull in a china shop!

BFFs: Heath Burns, Iris Clops

A-maze-ing
Manny's backpack and T-shirt are printed with a maze design. In Greek mythology, the Minotaur lived at the centre of a maze called the Labyrinth.

Blue jeans worn over sturdy brown boots

Star-crossed
Iris has hidden a love note in Manny's locker, reading "Got my eye on U". Inside, her romantic words reference the Taurus constellation, which represents the Minotaur.

Got my eye on U!

Pull

Dear Manny,

You are the only constellation in my midnight sky.

Love, Iris

IRIS CLOPS
One-eyed exclusive

Pattern on top looks like a bloodshot eye

Iris began her unlife as a background character in the Monster High webisodes and DVDs. However, the fans had their eye(s) on her and, at SDCC 2014, they finally got to see her incarnated in doll form.

Red flag to a bull
It was Draculaura who first encouraged Iris to talk to her crush, Manny. Unfortunately, Manny kept getting distracted by the colour red!

Oversized eye bag

Cropped black leggings

AGE:
15

DAUGHTER OF:
The Cyclops

KILLER STYLE:
Iris loves fabrics with watchful eye patterns on them.

FREAKY FLAW:
Iris is more than a little clumsy and doesn't always watch where she's going.

BFFs: Gigi Grant, Manny Taur

Pink high heels with vibrant eyes pattern

Pinned together
Iris may be a science nerd, but she likes to express her edgy side, too. She accessorizes her outfit with punky safety-pin earrings.

KIERAN VALENTINE
Forgiven vampire

Monster High has always been a place where ghouls and mansters could get a second chance, even if it's where they messed up their first one. Valentine is a former villain who once tried to steal Draculaura's heart, but at SDCC 2015 his redemption came in doll form, alongside wish-granting Djinni.

Embroidered roses on his jacket lapel

Waistcoat with brass buttons

Gold wallet chain

Lace-up, buckled riding boots

Summoning Djinni
While feeling sorry for himself and alone on the beach, Valentine spots a lamp half buried in the sand. When he rubs the seaweed off it, Djinni appears!

AGE:
1,602

SON OF:
Emo Vampires

KILLER STYLE:
Valentine never leaves his coffin without wearing his beast formalwear.

FREAKY FLAW:
Valentine lurks for love in the wrong places.

BFFs: Djinni "Whisp" Grant

Poetic licence
Valentine's jacket is embroidered with roses and petals on the sleeves, pockets and lapel, to reflect his sensitive and poetic (if somewhat self-centred) nature.

DJINNI "WHISP" GRANT
Genie of the lamp

Many people wish they could go back and right a wrong they committed, but sometimes not even a genie can make that wish come true. After she tried and failed to take over the world, it's something Djinni "Whisp" Grant understands all too well, although anyone who wished for her in doll form happily saw it granted at SDCC 2015.

Towering blue hairstyle

Moon phase tattoo on face

Blue and purple shoulder pads

Scorpion patterns on arms

Lower body is a whisp of smoke

Out and about
Djinni has a pair of legs that she can use when she wants to blend in with the other ghouls. Her shins have smokey markings on them and her pink shoes have curled toes.

AGE:
15

DAUGHTER OF:
A wish

KILLER STYLE:
Silk halter tops, baggy trousers and slippers

FREAKY FLAW:
Djinni used to want to rule the world, but the first step in fixing megalomania is recognising it, right?

BFFs: Kieran Valentine

HEXICIAH STEAM
Eccentric exclusive

Hexiciah was lost in the catacombs beneath Monster High for over 100 years. After being found by his daughter, Robecca, he chose SDCC as the place to make his first public appearance. Little did Hexiciah know that his old-fashioned style has a cool new name: steampunk.

Bushy grey moustache

Stylish silk cravat

Pinstripe detail on waistcoat

Hammer to tinker with inventions

Tool belt with extra tools

Forearm and hand are mechanical upgrades

Red breeches are gathered at knee

White stockings with bows on side

Brass-buckled shoes

FREAKY FACT
Hexiciah was one of the first monsters to theorise that the catacombs were created by an advanced race of monsters who mysteriously disappeared.

"It was then for a brief moment that I considered I must once again be dreaming, for coming towards me up the tunnel was Robecca."

AGE: Unknown, due to mechanical modifications

SON OF: A human father and fairy mother

KILLER STYLE: Old-school tailoring

FREAKY FLAW: Hexiciah's interest in the unknown often means he doesn't notice he's lost!

BFFs: Headless Headmistress Bloodgood

ROBECCA STEAM
Costumed in clockwork

Top hat with rivet details

Decorative metal hat pin

Student, scaredevil, Skultimate Roller Maze star, mechanical marvel, daughter; Robecca Steam is an analogue ghoul trying her beast to adapt to life in a digital world. This analog form of Robecca has no problem adapting to SDCC though, especially in her elaborate costume.

Gears in her eyes
It is possible to see the cogs whirring in Robecca's inventive mind, as her irises are shaped like metal gears.

Intricate chain belt made of spare parts

Brass printing on ruffled skirt

Copper skin polished to a shine

Studded shoes with ankle straps

"Next I knew, my feet were flying up the tunnel and into the arms of my father. Oh my gears...oh my gears..."

FREAKY FACT

Robecca took it upon herself to journey alone into the catacombs to find her father. Not only did she find Hexiciah, she found Cleo's long lost mother, too.

GLOSSCARY

The ghouls and mansters of Monster High have their own scary-cool way of speaking, which can take some getting used to for newcomers. Learn the students' lingo, including their everyday expressions and the names of their favourite places to fang out in.

VILE VOCABULARY

beast friend – best friend (also beasties for besties!)

boo love – true love

bootiful – beautiful

boovie – movie

clawesome – awesome

creeperific – terrific

creepover – sleepover

fanging out – hanging out

fangtastic – fantastic

ghoul – girl (also ghoul time for girl time)

ghoulfriend – girlfriend

haunt couture – haute couture

manster – male monster

maul – mall

monsturiser – moisturiser

normie – human, or "normal" person

scare and make-up – hair and make-up

scaritage – heritage

spooktacular – spectacular

unlife – life

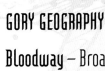

GORY GEOGRAPHY

Bloodway – Broadway

Boo Hexico – New Mexico

Boo Jersey – New Jersey

Boo York – New York

Costa Shrieka – Costa Rica

Goreway – Norway

Great Scarrier Reef – Great Barrier Reef

Hauntlywood – Hollywood

Hexico – Mexico

Londoom – London

Rotland – Scotland

Scaris – Paris (also known as the City of Frights)

Upper Beast Side – Upper East Side

SCHOOL SPEAK

casketball – basketball

fearleader – cheerleader

Home Ick – Home Economics

Ocean-ogre-phy – Oceanography

Physical Deaducation – Physical Education

scare-mester – semester

student disembody – student body

voltageous – electrifying

INDEX

Main entries are in **bold**.
Theme names are in *italic*.

DK | Penguin Random House

Senior Editor Hannah Dolan
Project Art Editor Lauren Adams
Editor Jo Casey
Designer Jenny Edwards
Pre-Production Producer Siu Yin Chan
Senior Producer Lloyd Robertson
Editorial Manager Paula Regan
Design Manager Guy Harvey
Art Director Lisa Lanzarini
Publisher Julie Ferris
Publishing Director Simon Beecroft

First published in Great Britain in 2016 by
Dorling Kindersley Limited
80 Strand, London WC2R 0RL
A Penguin Random House Company

10 9 8 7 6 5 4 3 2 1
001–283077–Sep/2016

Page design copyright © 2016 Dorling Kindersley Limited

A CIP catalogue record for this book
is available from the British Library.

ISBN: 978-0-24123-260-6

Printed in China

A WORLD OF IDEAS:
SEE ALL THERE IS TO KNOW

www.dk.com
www.mattel.com

ACKNOWLEDGEMENTS

DK would like to thank Charnita
Belcher, Nicole Corse, Ryan
Ferguson and Eric Hardie
at Mattel for all their help
in putting this book together.

Thanks also to Beth Davies,
David Fentiman and Helen
Murray at DK for additional
writing and editorial assistance;
and Jon Hall and Lisa Robb for
additional design work.

Finally, special thanks to Yvonne
Doyle for her clawesome
consultancy work and for allowing
us to borrow dolls from her
extensive collection.